STEVE MCQUEEN

W9-CDX-395

C I T Y P A C K
Los
Angeles

By Emma Stanford

Fodor's Travel Publications, Inc.
New York • Toronto • London • Sydney • Auckland

HTTP://WWW.FODORS.COM/

Contents

About this book

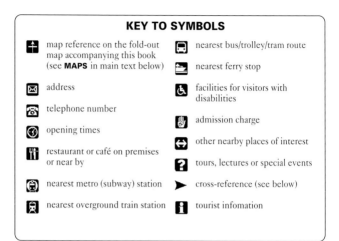

KEY TO SYMBOLS

✚	map reference on the fold-out map accompanying this book (see **MAPS** in main text below)	🚌	nearest bus/trolley/tram route
✉	address	🛥	nearest ferry stop
☎	telephone number	♿	facilities for visitors with disabilities
🕓	opening times	✋	admission charge
🍴	restaurant or café on premises or near by	⬌	other nearby places of interest
🚇	nearest metro (subway) station	❓	tours, lectures or special events
🚆	nearest overground train station	➤	cross-reference (see below)
		ℹ	tourist infomation

ORGANIZATION

Citypack Los Angeles' six sections cover the six most important aspects of your visit to Los Angeles.

- Los Angeles life—the city and its people
- Itineraries, walks and excursions—how to organize your time
- The top 25 sights to visit—from west to east across the city
- Features about different aspects of the city that make it special
- Detailed listings of restaurants, hotels, shops, and nightlife
- Practical information

In addition, text boxes provide fascinating extra facts and snippets, highlights of places to visit, and invaluable practical advice.

CROSS-REFERENCES

To help you make the most of your visit, cross-references, indicated by ➤ , show you where to find additional information about a place or subject.

MAPS

- **The fold-out map** in the wallet at the back of the book is a comprehensive street plan of central Los Angeles. Map references in the book such as J11 refer to this map. For example, the Natural History Museum at 900 Exposition Boulevard has the following information ✚ J11 indicating the grid square of the map in which the Natural History Museum will be found.
- **The maps on the inside front and back covers** of the book itself are for quick reference. They show Los Angeles and its surrounding area, and the Top 25 Sights, described on pages 24–48, are clearly plotted here by number (❶ – ㉕ , not page number) from west to east across the city.

PRICES

Where appropriate, an indication of the cost of an establishment is given by $ signs: **$$$** denotes higher than average prices, **$$** denotes average prices, **$** denotes lower than average charges. An indication of the admission charge (for all attractions) is given by categorizing the standard adult rate as follows: Expensive (over $15), Moderate (over $5), and Inexpensive ($5 and under).

LOS ANGELES *life*

INTRODUCING LOS ANGELES

Welcome to LaLaLand! A land of sunshine, promise and wealth beyond the dreams of avarice. Squeezed into a 1,000-square-mile basin encircled by picturesque mountains and the Pacific Ocean, this vast urban megalopolis is home to movie stars and Mickey Mouse, richly endowed art museums and surfer dudes. LA (locals never spell out "Los Angeles") is balanced on the cutting edge of cool, where restaurants, cars, pets, and people blister in and out of fashion in the blink of an eye. Tinseltown is also a master of illusion with a pedigree stretching back to the dawn of the Hollywood movie era. Behind the palm trees and the power lunches, there are earthquakes, mud slides, and grinding poverty —all part of the deal, and they lend LA an uncompromising edge far more realistic than the vicariously reported low-life dabblings of the Hollywood set.

Despite all that, the statistical likelihood of being caught in a major earthquake is remote. You are far more likely to suffer financially from valet parking, a legalized form of daylight robbery in a city that is landscaped by the combustion engine, where everybody drives everywhere.

Since 1781, when LA was founded by missionary farmers, the Downtown area has moved only a couple of blocks from the original site. Bounded by freeways, it remains the hub of the city, a highrise corporate ghetto where all eyes are focused on the burgeoning Pacific Rim market over the horizon. Beyond Downtown is Los Angeles County, made up of 88 incorporated cities and dozens of individual neighborhoods. On paper, it all looks like a cultural melting pot with the largest Hispanic and Asian/Pacific populations, and

Driving

The best way to get around LA is by car. And that means braving the freeways. Angelenos drive fast, change lanes more often than their socks, and cultivate a complete disregard for other traffic sharing the road. Not to worry, it's not as scary as it may seem. Still, do plan your trip in advance, leave plenty of time, and avoid rush hour periods and "car pool" lanes unless you have the requisite number of passengers.

Mural at Venice Beach

Downtown Los Angeles, backed by the San Gabriel Mountains

fourth largest African-American population in the United States. In reality, many neighborhoods are anything but a melting pot, and racial and ethnic tensions are always just below the surface.

Cut a broad swath west of Downtown to the Pacific shore at Santa Monica, and you will find the majority of the city's top sightseeing attractions, shopping, dining, and entertainment opportunities. Hollywood, West Hollywood, Beverly Hills, and West LA are the fickle heart of LaLaLand, where star-struck celebrities come out at night to watch each other in Spago or the Sky Bar, at the Viper Room, or the Improv. Of course, if you go and look for them, they are never there. The only way you can be sure of spotting celebrities in Tinseltown is to get a ticket for the *Tonight Show*.

However, if genuine stars are in short supply, there is nothing to prevent you from hamming it up in a dozen familiar-from-the-big- (or small-) screen locations, from Union Station (*Blade Runner*) and the Griffith Park Observatory (*Rebel without a Cause*) to Malibu (*Baywatch*, *The Rockford Files*). LA is definitely the place to indulge fantasies. Rent a limo for an evening out, wear sunglasses around the clock, hobnob with Goofy at Disneyland, and dress up for window shopping in Beverly Hills, then flounce into the Regent Beverly Wilshire (the *Pretty Woman* hotel) for a cocktail.

Literary LA

There is no better place to read Raymond Chandler's dark, gritty crime novels than in the city that inspired them in the 1930s and 1940s. Evelyn Waugh's satirical look at the American way of death, *The Loved One*, is based on LA's Forest Lawn Cemetery; Nathanael West rips into early Hollywood in *Day of the Locust*; and Hollywood insider and producer Julia Phillips lays bare "the industry" in modern times with *You'll Never Eat Lunch in This Town Again*.

7

A Day in the Life of Los Angeles

TGIF

Weekends in LA begin on a Friday night when Westwood Village goes pedestrian to cope with crowds sauntering between sidewalk cafés, cinemas, and record stores. Santa Monica's 3rd Street Promenade is another hot spot. Saturday is for shopping (➤ 70–77) and grooming (➤ 83) before the Big Night Out at Club… On Sunday mornings, brunch at the beach is an institution in the South Bay area, and no first-time visitor to LA should miss the colorful street parade that is Venice Beach each weekend.

They say nine out of ten Angelenos would prefer to live in Santa Monica. One of the chief charms of waking up in this oceanfront neighborhood is, of course, the beach, and in the misty early morning joggers and power walkers are already out pounding along the beach path.

By 7AM LA's 500 miles of freeway hell are clogging up. The average commuter drives a 30-mile roundtrip daily and, with coffee balanced on the dashboard and cellphone at the ready, trolls local radio stations in search of traffic information, weather conditions, and (in summer) the all-important smog report.

Angelenos "do" lunch from before noon to 1 or 2PM. Whether they grab a deli sandwich or graze on the latest in lettuce, mineral water is the typical accompaniment. Freeway mayhem reigns from around 3PM until 7PM, and by early evening the city's gyms are packed with lycra-clad bodies being honed to perfection.

Showered and refreshed, it might be time for a cocktail before dinner. LA's watering holes run the gamut from unpretentious bars to the rarified Polo Lounge, a renowned movie mogul haunt in the Beverly Hills Hotel. Shopping malls are busy in the evening, too, as shops stay open until 9 or 10. Westwood Village is a favorite place to catch dinner and a first-run movie; while the cultural classes might check out theater and concert listings in the *LA Weekly*. Melrose Avenue has hip eateries and comedy clubs but the poseurs' paradise is a sidewalk table on Sunset Plaza, ready to hit the Sunset Strip music club zone later.

Taking the dog for a walk, Venice Beach style

LOS ANGELES IN FIGURES

DISTANCES FROM DOWNTOWN
- Distance from San Francisco: 397 miles
- Distance from New York: 2,767 miles
- Distance from London: 5,460 miles
- Distance from San Andreas fault: 33 miles

AREA & POPULATION
- City of Los Angeles: 467 square miles/3.7 million people
- Los Angeles Five County Area: 34,149 square miles/14.5 million people
- Number of incorporated cities in the Five County Area: 88

GEOGRAPHY
- Latitude: 34° 04'N; longitude: 118° 15'W (roughly that of Atlanta, Casablanca, Beirut, Kashmir, and Osaka)
- Highest point: Mt. Wilson, 5,710 feet
- Lowest point: sea level
- Miles of shoreline in Five County Area: 160
- Miles of freeway: 528.3

WEATHER
- Warmest in July–August (average 83°/63°F max/min)
- Coolest in January (average 65°/45°F max/min)
- Wettest in February
- Average days of sunshine per annum: 329 (90 percent)
- Smog season: May–October
- LA's last snow fell on January 10, 1949 (³⁄₁₀ inch)

ENTERTAINMENT & ATTRACTIONS
- An average 50 productions are filmed daily on LA streets (▶ 52 Entertainment Industry Development Corporation)
- 1,100 LA theater productions sell 4 million tickets annually
- LA's film and TV industry employs 150,000 people
- More artists, writers, filmmakers, actors, dancers and musicians live and work in LA than in any other city at any other time in the history of civilization
- Annual movie industry receipts around $19 billion
- LA's No. 1 attraction: Universal Studios (Disneyland is No. 2)

A CHRONOLOGY

Pre-1781	Indian village of Yang-Na near Los Angeles River, close to present-day site of City Hall. Mission of San Gabriel Archangel founded 1771 in San Gabriel Valley (➤ 12)
1781	*Los Pobladores*, 44 farmer-settlers from the San Gabriel mission, establish El Pueblo de Nuestra Señora la Reina de Los Angeles in the fertile Los Angeles basin
1818	The Avila Adobe house is built for cattle rancher and mayor Don Francisco Avila
1825	California becomes a territory of Mexico
1842	Gold is discovered in the San Fernando Valley, six years before the discovery at Sutter's Mill that triggered the Gold Rush
1848	End of the Mexican–American War. California becomes part of the United States. (Achieves statehood 1850)
1872	The Southern Pacific Railroad Company commissions the first guidebook to Southern California. Charles Nordhoff's *California: For Health, Pleasure and Residence* creates a flood of visitors
1876	The first transcontinental railroad (Southern Pacific) arrives in Los Angeles
1880	The University of Southern California is founded with 53 students and 12 teachers
1881	General Harrison Gray Otis publishes the first issue of the *Los Angeles Times*
1888	The city's first African-American neighborhood is established at 1st and Los Angeles streets
1892	Edward Doheny discovers oil in Downtown
1902	LA's first movie house, the Electric Theatre, opens on Main Street

1909	Santa Monica Pier opens to attract tourists
1911	The Nestor Co. establishes Hollywood's first movie studio in the former Blondeau Tavern at Sunset and Gower
1913	Cecil B. De Mille makes Hollywood's first full-length feature film, *The Squaw Man*
1919	United Artists Film Corp founded by D.W. Griffith, Mary Pickford, Douglas Fairbanks, and Charlie Chaplin to improve actors' pay and working conditions
1927	The Academy of Motion Picture Arts and Sciences hosts first awards ceremony
1932	The Olympic Summer Games come to Exposition Park
1940	LA's first freeway, the Arroyo Seco Parkway
1955	Disneyland opens
1964	The Beatles perform at the Hollywood Bowl
1965	Race riots in Watts rage for six days leaving 34 dead and 1,032 wounded
1984	The Olympic Summer Games return to LA
1990	I.M. Pei's First Interstate World Center becomes the tallest building west of Chicago
1992	Riots follow acquittal of four White police officers accused of beating black motorist Rodney King (➤ 12)
1993	Brush fires threaten Malibu and cause more than $200 million worth of damage
1994	Northridge earthquake (6.8 on the Richter scale) kills 55 and does $30 billion damage
1997	Opening of the $1 billion Getty Center arts and cultural complex

PEOPLE & EVENTS FROM HISTORY

FATHER JUNÍPERO SERRA

Father Junípero Serra, a native of the Mediterranean island of Mallorca, was sent to Mexico to work as a missionary in 1749. In 1769, as Padre Presidente of the Spanish Franciscan missions in Baja (Lower) California, he accompanied the first governor of the Californias, Gaspar de Portolá, on a colonizing expedition to San Diego. Here they founded the first of 21 California missions in a chain that would reach from San Diego north to Sonoma. San Gabriel Archangel, in the San Gabriel Valley, was the fourth, built with the help of Native Americans, later known as Gabrieleno Indians.

D.W. GRIFFITH

David Wark Griffith (1875–1948) is often regarded as film-making's greatest pioneer and innovator. He began his career in New York, then moved to Los Angeles where he made *The Birth of a Nation* (banned in some cities for its racist tone), followed in 1916 by the lavish *Intolerance* starring Lillian Gish. Working with cameraman Billy Bitzer, Griffith experimented with lighting and camera techniques. An early champion of the "talkies," which he claimed would become "the greatest artistic medium the world has ever known," Griffith was also responsible for toning down the melodramatic proclivities of contemporary stage actors, adapting their style for film.

THE 1992 LA RIOTS

When the videotaped 1991 beating of black motorist Rodney King by white LAPD officers failed to secure a single court conviction, racial tensions among LA's African-American community exploded in the country's most destructive episode of civil unrest this century. The first outbreak of violence came within hours of the not-guilty verdicts being delivered on April 29 1992. Some 48 hours later, 52 people were dead, 2,400 injured, 1,600 businesses were closed for good, and property damage exceeded $1 billion.

The Los Angeles Aqueduct

As LA boomed around the turn of the 20th century, the demand for water became a major issue. When water bureau superintendent William Mulholland suggested an aqueduct to transport melted snow from the Sierra Nevadas to feed the growing city, he was thought to be mad. However, Mulholland's aqueduct, all 223 miles and 142 tunnels of it, opened in 1913, and with a 105-mile extension into the Mono Basin, it still supplies the city. Roman Polanksi's *Chinatown* dramatizes the early struggles in the area over water.

D.W. Griffith directing
Battle of the Sexes

LOS ANGELES
how to organize your time

ITINERARIES

Los Angeles is so vast it makes sense to sightsee neighborhood by neighborhood, and a car is almost essential. It is a good idea to check the map in advance and plot a route. Except Downtown, parking is easy and inexpensive.

ITINERARY ONE	**HOLLYWOOD BOULEVARD TO HOLLYHOCK HOUSE**
Morning	Start off outside Mann's Chinese Theater (➤ 55), then cross the street to the Hollywood Roosevelt Hotel (➤ 53) for a Hollywood history lesson. Stop by the Hollywood Entertainment Museum (➤ 53), Hollywood Guinness World of Records Museum (➤ 58) and Frederick's of Hollywood Lingerie Museum (➤ 52).
Lunch	Celebrity-spot at Musso & Frank Grill (➤ 81), or picnic in Barnsdall Park at Hollyhock House (➤ 34). Late lunchers will find plenty of options on Melrose Avenue (➤ 70).
Afternoon	After a tour of Hollyhock House (➤ 34), take a detour via the Hollywood Memorial Park Cemetery (➤ 52) to Melrose Avenue (➤ 70).
ITINERARY TWO	**SOUTH BAY (PALOS VERDES TO LONG BEACH)**
Morning	Take the scenic route around the Palos Verdes headland (off the Pacific Coast Highway) via Lloyd Wright's Wayfarer's Chapel to San Pedro and the Los Angeles Maritime Museum (➤ 50). Kids might enjoy the free Cabrillo Aquarium (➤ 59) near by. The Banning Residence Museum (➤ 50) is en route to Long Beach and the *Queen Mary* (➤ 42). This is a good place to stop for lunch.
Lunch	Belmont Brewing Company (➤ 69).
Afternoon	The Long Beach Aquarium of the Pacific is a couple of minutes from Downtown. A 10-minute drive west, Rancho Los Alamitos, a turn-of-the-century landmark (➤ 43), is a delight.

ITINERARY THREE	PASADENA

Morning

The Huntington (➤ 46) does not open until noon on weekdays except in summer. However, Pasadena has much else to offer starting with the historic Mission San Gabriel Archangel (➤ 56). The Los Angeles State and County Arboretum (➤ 47) is a real treat, and the Descanso Gardens (➤ 57) are famous for camellias (Jan–Mar). Then head for Old Town Pasadena (➤ 70).

Lunch

Colorado Boulevard's Pasadena Baking Company (➤ 69) or nextdoor neighbor Mia Piace are two good options. Also the Gordon Biersch Brewery (➤ 67) and The Raymond (➤ 62).

Afternoon

Visit the Huntington. Afterwards tour the stunning Gamble House (➤ 44; closes at 3) or visit the Norton Simon Museum of Art (➤ 45). Both are open afternoons only, Thursday to Sunday.

ITINERARY FOUR	SANTA MONICA TO VENICE BEACH

Morning

Hit the stores at Third Street Promenade and Santa Monica Place (➤ 70–71). Then head straight for Santa Monica Pier (➤ 24), where you can rent a bike for the day and coast down the beach bike path with detours off to shops and galleries on Main Street (between Hollister and Rose avenues), also home to architect Frank Gehry's Edgemar development ✉ **2435 Main** and the California Heritage Museum ✉ **2612 Main**

Lunch

Try the terrace at Rockenwagner (➤ 67), the patio of the World Café (➤ 68), or Venice's beachfront Sidewalk Café (➤ 68) for excellent people-watching.

Afternoon

Hit the beach after lunch. Or take a stroll around the canal district (➤ 24); stop by the landmark Chiat/Day Inc Advertising Building (➤ 54); and visit the Museum of Flying (➤ 58).

WALKS

AROUND DOWNTOWN: PERSHING SQUARE TO LITTLE TOKYO

Start off at Pershing Square with its purple bell-tower and multicolored building block art installations, then cut through the sumptuously refurbished Biltmore Hotel to Grand Avenue. (The LA Conservancy's guided walking tours depart from the Biltmore on Saturdays ➤ 19) Take a turn around the Los Angeles Central Library, then, across 5th Street, climb the Bunker Hill Steps from the foot of the First Interstate World Center.

All aboard Angel's Flight

Bunker Hill At the top of the city's glass-canyoned Financial District, the Wells Fargo History Museum is just across the road from the Museum of Contemporary Art (MOCA) and California Plaza. The Plaza is a good place to catch your breath and watch the dancing fountains before taking the Angel's Flight funicular down to Grand Central Market. Walk through the market and cross Broadway to the Bradbury Building, near the corner with 3rd Street.

Coffee breaks There are several sidewalk café-coffee shops on the Bunker Hill Steps and at the Wells Fargo center, plus the upscale cafeteria Patinette at MOCA ✉ 250 S Grand Avenue ☎ 213/626–1178.

Little Tokyo Shuttle bus DASH D operates from Spring Street (one block east on 3rd Street) to Union Station, passing within a block of Little Tokyo. You could also walk to 2nd Street (one block north), then east for Japanese Village Plaza.

Time for lunch Grand Central Market is a great place to eat cheaply; bakers, fruit sellers, and deli stalls offer everything from tacos to Chinese noodles. Near Union Station is Philippe The Original (➤ 69) for sandwiches; on Olvera Street there are plenty of Mexican restaurants, including La Golondrina (➤ 66).

THE SIGHTS

INFORMATION

Distance approx 1½ miles
Time 2–3 hours
Start point Pershing Square
✚ M7
🚇 Pershing Square
🚍 DASH B, C, E
End point Little Tokyo
✚ N7
🚍 DASH A, D

AROUND EL PUEBLO: UNION STATION TO CHINATOWN

Take time to explore inside the splendid Spanish Colonial-style Union Station building before walking up to the Old Plaza at the heart of El Pueblo de Los Angeles, the center of the original settlement here. The tree-shaded plaza is flanked by historic buildings including the 1870 Pico House built by the last Mexican governor of California.

Olvera Street Stroll down this restored 19th-century street, tightly packed with the souvenir and craft stalls of a Mexican street market wedged between historic brick façades. Here lively sidewalk restaurants, takeout taco stands, and ice-cream and *churros* vendors do a swift trade. Stop off at the city's oldest dwelling, the Avila Adobe, which was founded in 1818 and has since been much enlarged. The Visitor Information Center, located in the Sepulveda House, presents a short video showing a brief history of Los Angeles.

Avila Adobe, the city's oldest home

Chinatown Walk west a couple of blocks to Broadway, then north. Though no match for San Francisco's bustling Chinatown, the 900 block of Broadway boasts a handful of Asian-inspired bank buildings in the Bank of America, the East-West Bank, guarded by stone lion-dogs, and the United Savings Bank on the corner of Sun-Yat-Sen Plaza, where there is a well-used wishing-well. Around the plaza are restaurants, fortune tellers, and shops selling a wide assortment of wares including incense, jade carvings, pottery, and plum sauce.

THE SIGHTS

- Union Station (► 56)
- El Pueblo de Los Angeles Historic Park and Olvera Street (► 41)

INFORMATION

Distance approx 1¼ miles
Time 1½–2 hours
Start point Union Station
➕ N6
🚉 Union Station
🚌 DASH B, D
End point Chinatown
➕ N5
🚌 DASH B

17

EVENING STROLLS

Although LA is a car town, there are a couple of pedestrian-friendly enclaves where a pre-prandial stroll is in order.

OLD PASADENA

Perfect for a gentle amble combined with a bit of window-shopping (▶ 70), this three-block section of Colorado Boulevard, in one of LA's most affluent suburbs, also offers a wide choice of restaurants. Admire the handsome old brick buildings ornamented with decorative reliefs and wrought ironwork.

OLVERA STREET

El Pueblo's Mexican street market continues well into the evening. Souvenir-hunting followed by people-watching over pre-dinner margaritas is a pastime of visitors here.

SANTA MONICA

Watch the sunset from the pier, then stroll to pedestrianized 3rd Street Promenade, edged by dozens of bars, cafés, shops, and restaurants, which stay open late.

WESTWOOD VILLAGE

The magic triangle of Westwood Boulevard, Broxton, and Weyburn avenues on the southern edge of the UCLA campus was actually designed to be pedestrian-friendly, a rare quality in LA. The architecture is 1920s Mediterranean Revival; sidewalk cafés, coffee bars, restaurants, and movie theaters abound.

INFORMATION

Old Pasadena
Start point Between Arroyo
    Parkway and Delacey
    Avenue
➕ Off map, northeast
🚌 180, 181, 484

Olvera Street
Start point Old Plaza, El Pueblo
    de Los Angeles
➕ N6
🚉 Union Station
🚌 DASH B, D

Santa Monica
Start point Santa Monica Pier
➕ Off map, west
🚌 22, 322, 434, SM1, SM7,
    SM10

Westwood Village
Start point Westwood Boulevard
    (off Wilshire)
➕ Off map, west
🚌 20, 21, 22, 320, 322, SM1,
    SM2, SM3

*The pier at Santa Monica
is a favorite filming
location*

ORGANIZED SIGHTSEEING

WALKING TOURS

Los Angeles Conservancy ☎ 213/623–2489
Excellent Saturday morning Downtown walking tours with options ranging from historic Broadway theaters to art deco architecture.

JRT International—"Hiking in L.A."
☎ 818/501–1005 Scenic hiking tours with an educational angle in the Santa Monica Mountains.

BUS TOURS

Hollywood Fantasy Tours ☎ 323/469–8184 The classic star tours covering the famous and infamous sites and movie star homes of Hollywood and Beverly Hills.

Oskar J's Sightseeing Tours ☎ 818/501–2217 A wide range of options including bus tours around Hollywood celebrity haunts and houses, helicopter tours, and harbor cruises.

LIMOUSINE TOURS

Star Limousine Tours ☎ 310/829–1066 and **Ultra Tours** ☎ 310/274–1303 both offer tours of star homes and other Hollywood landmarks in stretch-limo luxury.

HELICOPTER TOURS

Heli U.S.A. Helicopters ☎ 310/641–9494 A great romantic nighttime package with a spectacular flight over the city followed by dinner at DC3 (► 67). Also daytime flights.

Island Express Helicopters ☎ 310/510–2525 The fastest route to Catalina Island (► 20) from Long Beach and San Pedro, plus sightseeing, sunset, dinner and heli-golfing packages.

BOAT TRIPS

Gondola Getaway ☎ 562/433–9595 BYO champagne and the stripey-shirted gondolier will provide ice bucket, glasses and hors d'oeuvres to accompany a Venetian-style gondola ride around the canals of Naples Island (Long Beach).

Shoreline Village Cruises ☎ 562/495–5884 Summer season harbor cruises and whale-watching expeditions (Jan–Apr) from Long Beach. Guaranteed whale sightings, or second trip for free.

NBC Studio tours

The only LA television studio to offer tours, NBC Studio (✉ 3000 W Alameda Avenue, Burbank ☎ 818/840–3537), invites visitors to take a look around its broadcasting complex. Check out the wardrobe and make-up departments, visit a special effects set and *The Tonight Show* set. Free tickets for that evening's show of the talkfest that Johnny Carson made famous are available at the Studio's ticket counter. Get there early.

EXCURSIONS

HIKING IN THE SANTA MONICA MOUNTAINS

One mile west of the Getty Museum, Topanga Canyon Boulevard climbs up from the Malibu seashore into the foothills of the Santa Monica Mountains. As it passes through the laid-back alternative community of Topanga Canyon, bear right on Entrada Road, signposted for Topanga State Park. Trails criss-cross the 9,000-acre chaparral reserve, winding through oak and sumac woodlands and across rolling pastures with views of the mountains and off to the ocean. Watch for red-tailed hawks wheeling overhead, California quail, and even the occasional roadrunner.

Solstice Canyon Park, a former ranch off the Pacific Coast Highway just west of Malibu, is reckoned to have one of the finest walking trails in the mountains. There are two routes that form a convenient loop from the car park: the gentle 1½-mile Solstice International Trail, which is shady in summer, along an old ranch road to a waterfall grotto fed by Solstice Creek; and the connecting Rising Sun Trail, a 3-mile high chaparral hike with notable views.

CATALINA ISLAND

An idyllic island 26 miles off the coast, Catalina offers lovely beaches, great diving, a miraculously undeveloped interior, and a herd of buffalo introduced when filming *The Vanishing American* in 1925. Take the Catalina Cruises ferry (1 hour 50 minutes), the catamaran (under an hour), or the Catalina Express hydrofoil (1 hour 10 minutes) to Avalon, and drop in at the Chamber of Commerce office on the pier for a map, and sightseeing, glass-bottomed boat, horse-riding, and dive tour information (also hiking permits). Explore the pretty main town of Avalon, stopping off at the marvelous 1920s Casino and the Catalina Museum, then climb the hill to the Zane Grey Pueblo Hotel (➤ 85) for the harbor view. The cheap Catalina Safari Bus stops at beaches, trails and campgrounds en route to Two Harbors resort village. An overnight stay is highly recommended; make a reservation well in advance.

MISSION SAN JUAN CAPISTRANO

The seventh of the California missions, San Juan Capistrano was founded in 1776. The picturesque ruins of the Stone Church are home to the famous swallows that are said to return here from Argentina for the summer every March 19. Take time to wander in the pretty gardens, shaded by jacaranda trees and bright in season with camellias, roses, hibiscus, and bougainvilleas. There is a blacksmith's shop and restored bar-rack buildings housing Spanish-era artifacts, plus the lovely painted adobe Serra Chapel. Beyond the mission, the town has Spanish-style buildings and several antiques stores on Camino Capistrano, plus a local history museum, across the he railroad tracks.

The two main driving routes south to San Juan are the fast, direct I-5/Santa Ana Freeway (about an hour from Downtown to the I-74 exit) and the Pacific Coast Highway, passing through Huntington, Newport, and Laguna Beaches. It's slower, but it's spectacular seaside vistas, farther north especially, make it one of the most famous drives in the world.

INFORMATION

Mission San Juan Capistrano
- ✉ Ortega Highway
- ☎ 714/248–2049
- 🕐 Daily 8:30–5
- 🚊 Trains from Union Station
- 💲 Inexpensive

San Juan Capistrano

J. PAUL GETTY MUSEUM, MALIBU

Since 1997 the new Getty Center (➤ 25) has housed the bulk of the Getty collections while the Malibu site is renovated before reopening in 2001 as a showcase for the Getty antiquities. The superb displays of Greek and Roman art will be housed in the reconstruction of a Roman villa based on the Villa dei Papyri, which was destroyed by the eruption of Mount Vesuvius in AD 79.

J. Paul Getty Museum
- ➕ Off map, west
- ✉ 17985 Pacific Coast Highway
- ☎ Information: 310/458–2003

WHAT'S ON

For up-to-date details, check with the Los Angeles Convention and Visitor Bureau Events Hotline ☎ 213/689–8822. The multilingual service lists local happenings. The Calendar section of Sunday's *Los Angeles Times* provides a weekly guide, as does the free *LA Weekly*.

JANUARY   *Rose Parade*: Pasadena's New Year's Day spectacular features marching bands and extravagant floats, along with the Rose Bowl football game

FEBRUARY   *Chinese New Year*: A Golden Dragon Parade winds its way through Chinatown

MARCH   *Academy Awards*: Celebrities gather Downtown

MAY   *Cinco de Mayo*: Mexicans celebrate Mexico's independence from France (1867) with feasting, music and dance. Olvera Street is a good place to join in the fun

JUNE   *Gay and Lesbian Pride Celebration*: Massive weekend event held around West Hollywood Park. Also in June, the Annual Mariachi-USA Festival at the Hollywood Bowl

JULY   *Hollywood Bowl Summer Festival*: Evening open-air concerts with broad-ranging program—classical music, jazz, and pops (July–September)

AUGUST   *Nisei Week*: Dance and martial arts demonstrations, crafts and food stalls as Little Tokyo celebrates Japanese-American cultural heritage

OCTOBER   *AFI Film Festival*: The American Film Institute descends on LA for a two-week independent and foreign film binge

NOVEMBER   *Dia de los Muertos*: Folklorico musicians, puppet shows, Mexican music and crafts on Olvera Street for the Day of the Dead
Doo Dah Parade: Pasadena's irreverent Rose Parade spoof

DECEMBER   *Hollywood Christmas Parade*: Major floats, marching bands, classic cars, celebrity guests

LOS ANGELES'
top 25 sights

*The sights are shown on the maps on the inside front cover and inside back cover, numbered **1–25** from west to east across the city*

SANTA MONICA & VENICE BEACH

HIGHLIGHTS

- Main Street galleries and restaurants
- Muscle Beach
- Natural Elements Sculpture Park (south of the pier)
- Ocean Front Walk
- Pacific Coast Bike Path
- Santa Monica Pier
- Sunset from Palisades Park, on Ocean Avenue, by Santa Monica and Wilshire boulevards
- 3rd Street Promenade
- Venice Canal Walkway (access from S Venice Boulevard)

INFORMATION

- Inside front cover
- Santa Monica Visitor Center, 1400 Ocean Avenue (between Santa Monica Boulevard and Colorado Avenue)
- 310/393–7593
- Daily 10–4 (until 5 in summer)
- 4, 20, 22, 33, 304, 320, 333
- Good to non-existent depending on location
- J Paul Getty Museum (➤ 20)
  Chiat/Day Inc Advertising Building (➤ 54)
  Will Rogers State Historic Park (➤ 57)
  Museum of Flying (➤ 58)
  Bergamot Station (➤ 74)
- Walking tours of Santa Monica murals:
  310/822–9560

The beach, the palm trees, people–watching on Ocean Front Walk, plus great shopping and dining, make these seaside haunts enduringly popular.

Pier pressure Santa Monica's landmark 1909 pier still exudes that old-fashioned amusement-park aura which evokes a fuzzy nostalgia in adults and requests for money from attendant offspring. Along the weathered wooden boardwalk, Pacific Park's (➤ 58) giant Ferris wheel and roller-coaster loom above the restored 1922 carousel operated by Paul Newman in *The Sting*. Down at beach level, the UCLA Ocean Discovery Center presents marine exhibits, aquariums and touch tanks. You can also rent a bike or in-line skates to swoop along the 26-mile concrete beach path.

Beyond the beach Santa Monica's inland entertainment hub is 3rd Street Promenade, four pedestrianized blocks of shops, cafés, and movie theaters. For a more esoteric experience, check out Main Street (between Hollister and Rose Avenues), with its trendy restaurants and art galleries, and the California Heritage Museum (at Ocean Park), housed in an 1894 residence built for Santa Monica's founder, Senator John Jones (➤ 15).

Venice Beach Where Main crosses Rose Street, Joseph Borofsky's *Ballerina Clown* figure greets visitors to Venice. It is an appropriate icon for this entertaining beach community, a throwback to the psychedelic Sixties combined with the narcissism of Muscle Beach. Ocean Front Walk is where it all hangs out, a nonstop parade of scantily clad humanity, body-builders, singers, and stalls. Just inland, the Venice Canal Walkway explores the quiet canal-lined residential neighborhood that gave the area its name.

2

THE GETTY CENTER

Carved into the foothills of West LA's Santa Monica Mountains, Richard Meier's magnificent Getty Center has quickly become LA's most impressive architectural and cultural landmark.

The background Oil billionaire J. Paul Getty began collecting in the 1930s and a passion for Greek and Roman antiquities inspired the J. Paul Getty Museum at Malibu (► 21). After his death (1976) and $700 million bequest, the size of its collections swelled. Opened in 1997, the $1 billion Getty Center houses this trove of 13th- to 19th-century Western art as well as the J. Paul Getty Trust's arts education, research, and funding programs.

Treasure Part fortress, part piazza, and focus of the 24-acre complex, the stunning inside-out architecture is a triumph. Five honey-colored pavilions flank the central courtyard. The first four display the collections in chronological order; decorative arts and sculpture are on the ground floor and paintings from the corresponding period on the upper level; the fifth pavilion houses special exhibitions.

First you will see medieval and Renaissance works, from the Ludwig illuminated manuscripts to the works of Fra Angelico. Next, stroll by the Old Masters—works by Brueghel, Rembrandt, Rubens, and Van Dyck. There are also splendid English portraits, grand galleries of 18th-century French decorative arts, and memorable 19th-century images, from Civil War photographs to Van Gogh's *Irises*. Step outside for a break in an outdoor café or to explore the gardens, whose elegant geometric plantings have a distinctly Zen feel. The Getty's one drawback is its popularity.

HIGHLIGHTS

- Ludwig Manuscripts
- Old Master Gallery
- French decorative arts
- *Irises*, Van Gogh

INFORMATION

- ✚ Inside front cover
- ✉ 1200 Getty Center Drive, off I–405/San Diego Freeway
- ☎ 310/440–7300
- ⏰ Tue–Wed 11–7; Thu–Fri 11–9; Sat–Sun 10–6. Closed Mon and public holidays

Top: Coronation of the Virgin, *da Fabriano. Above:* Bacchante, *ter Brugghen*

- 🍴 Restaurant ($$; reservations essential) and cafés ($)
- 🚌 561, SM14. Ask driver for free admission pass
- ♿ Excellent
- 💲 Museum: free. Parking: inexpensive (reservations essential)
- ❓ Audioguides, talks, concerts

25

ARMAND HAMMER MUSEUM OF ART

HIGHLIGHTS

- *Beach at Trouville,* Boudin
- *Dans l'Omnibus,* Vuillard
- *Grunwald Center exhibitions*
- *Hospital at Saint-Rémy,* Van Gogh
- *Mme Hessel at the Seashore,* Vuillard
- *The Sower,* Van Gogh
- *Street Scene,* Bonnard

INFORMATION

- ⊞ Inside front cover
- ✉ 10899 Wilshire Boulevard, Westwood
- ☎ 310/443–7000
- 🕐 Tue–Sat 11–7 (Thu 11–9); Sun 11–6. Closed Mon
- 🍴 Courtyard café (S)
- 🚌 20, 21, 22, 320
- ♿ Very good
- 💲 Inexpensive
- ↔ Westwood Village (➤ 18 and 70)
  UCLA's Franklin D. Murphy Sculpture Garden (➤ 59)

Above: Two Actors,
Honoré Daumier
*Right: bust of
Armand
Hammer*

Roundly criticized for its architecture, the lack of "importance" of its collections, even for its existence, the Hammer is not a big favorite with the local cultural panjandrums. However, there are several worthwhile small-scale treasures here.

Hammer and tongs Much of the highbrow carping about the Hammer is probably sour grapes. The immensely rich and acquisitive Armand Hammer, an oil millionaire many times over, originally promised his art collections to a number of local institutions. When he decided to build his own museum instead, the news was greeted with dismay.

Minor miracles Modest in size, the Hammer is a respite from more overwhelming local museums. Its collection is comprised mainly of Impressionist and Post-Impressionist works by painters such as Monet, Pissarro, and Mary Cassatt; complementary works from UCLA's own collections are also shown here.

Changing exhibitions Selections from the 19th-century Daumier and His Contemporaries Collection, featuring paintings, sculpture, and lithographs by the leading French satirist of the age, are shown in rotation. The museum is also a showcase for the UCLA Grunwald Center for the Graphic Arts. This collection of more than 35,000 prints, drawings, photographs, and book illustrations, containing works by such luminaries as Dürer, Cézanne, Matisse, and Jasper Johns, is displayed in other themed exhibitions. It is worth checking out the museum's temporary program.

BEVERLY HILLS

Love it or loathe it, you can't say you've "done Los Angeles" until you've seen Beverly Hills. The city's most recognizable zip code (90210) is also LA's most visited neighborhood, receiving over 14 million visitors a year.

A star is born In a classic rags-to-riches story, the countrified suburb of Beverly Hills, west of Hollywood, was plucked from obscurity by the movies—Douglas Fairbanks Jr. to be exact, who set up home here in 1919, followed by Charlie Chaplin, Gloria Swanson, and Rudolph Valentino.

The Golden Triangle Today, Beverly Hills remains ostentatiously star-studded, a monument to conspicuous consumption. For black-belt window shopping, there's the Golden Triangle, bounded by Crescent Drive and Wilshire and Santa Monica boulevards and bisected by world-famous Rodeo Drive, a showpiece three-block strip of designer emporiums. At the Wilshire Boulevard end, the $200-million self-proclaimed "European-style" Via Rodeo fashion retail complex features real cobblestones, a miniaturized version of Rome's Spanish Steps, and the busiest branch of jewelers Tiffany & Co. outside Manhattan.

Seeing the sights A historical Beverly Hills walking tour map is available from the Visitors Bureau. The walk takes about two hours and covers such local sights as the imposing City Hall, Beverly Gardens, and the wonderful Gaudí-like O'Neill House ☒ 507 N Rodeo Drive (go down the alley to admire the swirling stucco and mosaic inlay of the guest house). If you want to see movie-moguls at play, try the Polo Lounge at the flamingo pink Beverly Hills Hotel (▶ 84).

DID YOU KNOW?

- Beverly Hills covers a mere 5.69 square miles
- The average net annual income of Beverly Hills households is $121,396
- Beverly Hills' 417 licensed beauty, health, and hair-styling businesses generate over $50 million per annum
- The Rodeo Drive boutique featured in Judith Krantz's *Scruples* was based on Fred Hayman, 273 N Rodeo Drive
- Beverly Hills' original star mansion was Pickfair, the home of Douglas Fairbanks and Mary Pickford at 1143 Summit Drive

INFORMATION

Beverly Hills Visitors Bureau
- ✚ Inside front cover
- ☒ 239 S Beverly Drive
- ☎ 310/271–8174
- ◉ Mon–Fri 8:30–5
- ▤ 20, 21, 22, 320, 322

Beverly Hills Trolley Tour
- ☒ Rodeo Drive at Dayton Way
- ☎ 310/285–2563
- ◉ Jul–Labor Day daily, hourly departures noon–5; May–Jun, Sep–Nov Sat only noon–4. Tour duration 40 minutes
- ⓘ Inexpensive
- ⬌ Museum of Television and Radio (▶ 51) Greystone Park (▶ 57) Virginia Robinson Gardens (▶ 57)

LA COUNTY MUSEUM OF ART

HIGHLIGHTS

- Drawings and pastels, Degas
- Edo scrolls and netsuke, Japanese Pavilion
- Moscow Avant-Garde School paintings and drawings (Kandinsky and Rodchenko)
- *Jazz Facsimile*, Matisse
- *La Pipe*, Magritte
- Persian illuminated manuscripts
- *Untitled*, Rothko
- *Waterlilies*, Monet

INFORMATION

- Inside front cover
- 5905 Wilshire Boulevard, Midtown
- 323/857-6010
- Mon, Tue, Thu noon–8; Fri noon–9; Sat–Sun 11–8. Closed Wed, Thanksgiving, Christmas
- Plaza Café (S–SS)
- 20, 21, 22, 217, 320, 322
- Very good
- Moderate
- Petersen Automotive Museum (➤ 29)
  George C. Page Museum of La Brea (➤ 50)
  Farmers' Market (➤ 71)

Portrait of an Artist (Pool with Two Figures), *David Hockney*

28

One of the finest, most broad-ranging art museums in the United States, LACMA also draws kudos alfresco jazz concerts in the courtyard plaza on Friday evenings and Sunday afternoons.

The collections The majority of the museum's permanent collections are housed in the Ahmanson Building. Here magnificent examples of ancient Asian, Egyptian, and pre-Columbian art, medieval and Renaissance paintings, works by 17th-century Dutch landscape specialists and 18th-century French Romantics have been gathered together with a feast of Impressionist, Fauvist, Cubist, and Surrealist art. There is a dazzling array of British silver, diverse examples of European and American decorative arts, plus costumes and textiles, jewel-like Persian manuscripts, and Ottoman ceramics. The museum boasts world-class collections of 20th-century German and German Expressionist art, and the Bruce Goff Japanese Pavilion is a work of art in itself.

Exhibitions and sculpture gardens In addition to housing selections from the permanent collections, the Anderson and Hammer Buildings offer acres of special exhibition space, and LACMA is a great place to catch top-flight visiting exhibitions. The buildings are flanked by sculpture gardens with works by Rodin, Bourdelle, Calder, and Alice Aycock.

Make a plan The museum complex is spread over five buildings. Its collections are so vast and varied that there is far too much to be seen comfortably in a single visit, so it is advisable to plot a route around personal favorites with the aid of a layout plan (constantly changing) from the information booth.

PETERSEN AUTOMOTIVE MUSEUM

What better place to examine the cult of the automobile than Los Angeles, a city entirely shaped by the motor car?

Driving through history The largest museum of its kind in the US, the Petersen explores automotive history and culture from early jalopies to the sleek dream machines of the Testa Rossa zone. The ground-floor "Streetscape," a series of dioramas and eye-catching displays designed to illustrate the effects of motoring on people's lives, kicks off with a 1911 American Underslung touring car puffing real steam from its radiator, and continues via a classic Laurel and Hardy scene involving a Ford Model T, to a gleaming 1929 gas station, and a glossy 1930s new car showroom complete with cigar-chomping buyer. "L.A. Autotude" salutes the automobile as fashion accessory with a selection of bizarre and eccentric cars off the city's streets, and there are tributes to the 1950s and '60s, plus a look at vehicles of the future.

HIGHLIGHTS

- Vintage cars
- Cars of the Stars
- Californian customized cars

INFORMATION

- Inside front cover
- 6060 Wilshire Boulevard, Midtown
- 323/930–2277
- Daily 10–6 (Fri until 9PM)
- Cafeteria (S)
- 20, 21, 22, 217, 320, 322
- Very good
- Moderate
- LA County Museum of Art (➤ 28)
  George C. Page Museum of La Brea (➤ 50)
  Farmers' Market (➤ 71)

Capital of customizing On the second floor, the galleries present a constantly changing feast of automotive excellence: stars' cars in the Hollywood Gal-lery; LA hot rods from California's capital of customizing; and the Otis Chandler Motor-cycle Gallery.

Top: diorama of 1911 touring car. Right: car showroom, 1930s

HOLLYWOOD BOULEVARD

INFORMATION

Visitors Information Center

- E1
- Janes House, 6541 Hollywood Boulevard, Hollywood
- 213/689–8822 (Events Hotline)
- Mon–Sat 9–5. Closed Sun
- 1, 217
- Free
- Hollyhock House (➤ 34), Frederick's of Hollywood Lingerie Museum (➤ 52), Hollywood Memorial Park Cemetery (➤ 52), Capitol Records Tower (➤ 54)

Above: Mann's Chinese Theater. Below: the famous hand- and footprints outside it

Though Hollywood Boulevard's 1930s and 1940s heyday is a distant memory, movie buffs can still get a kick out of inspecting Trigger's hoofprints outside Mann's Chinese Theater.

Facelift After almost 50 years of decay and decline, Tinseltown's most evocative address is undergoing a major facelift. One of the first things to be buffed up along the boulevard has been the Hollywood Walk of Fame. Stretching between Gower Street and La Brea Avenue, with an annex on Vine, almost 2,000 bronze stars set in the sidewalk honor celebrities in film, television, theater, and radio. The select few invited to place their hands, feet, hooves, or (in the case of Betty Grable) legs in the concrete courtyard of Mann's Chinese Theater (➤ 55) include Joan Crawford, James Stewart, and Cary Grant. Here, booths sell self-guided Hollywood star site maps; Grave Line Tours (➤ 53) are the best insider guide to Hollywood deviancy and shenanigans.

Hollywood history Sid Grauman, who built the Chinese Theater, was also one of the founding partners in the Hollywood Roosevelt Hotel (➤ 53) across the street. A couple of Michelle Pfeiffer's nightclub scenes from *The Fabulous Baker Boys* were filmed here. The Hollywood Enertainment Museum (➤ 53) is an interesting stop near by; an assortment of celebrity figures peoples the Hollywood Wax Museum ✉ 6767 Hollywood Boulevard ⏰ daily until midnight, while kids might enjoy the Hollywood Guinness World of Records Museum (➤ 58).

UNIVERSAL STUDIOS

The world's biggest and busiest motion picture and television studio-cum-theme park is a great family day out. Indeed for many visitors, the classic **Back To The Future** *and more recent* **Jurassic Park** *are alone worth the cost of admission.*

Back to the beginning Universal Studios' founder Carl Laemmle moved his movie studio facility to the Hollywood Hills in 1915 and inaugurated Universal Studios tours during the silent movie era. The arrival of the talkies put an end to live audiences until 1964, when trolley tours began; trolleys are still used to circle the 415-acre backlot.

Orientation To get the most out of your day, pick up a copy of the daily schedule at the entrance; it lists the various shows and attractions. At the top of everyone's list is the Backlot Tour—the latest incarnation of the tour that started it all—which includes close encounters with old banana breath himself in *Kongfrontation*, Jaws snapping his way around Amity Harbor, the ground-trembling *Earthquake: The Big One*, and classic locations from the *Psycho* house to the Little Europe Streetscape. Trolley tours depart from the Upper Lot, which is also home to the thrilling *Back to the Future* simulator ride and half-a-dozen great shows and revues including the distinctly gunky and slimy kid's TV favorite, *Totally Nickelodeon*.

Take a ride A quarter-mile escalator links the Upper Lot to the Lower Lot, the heart of the working studio complex. Here Universal's $100 million *Jurassic Park—The Ride* adventure visits a land of five-story dinosaurs built with the help of aerospace scientists. There are red hot special effects at the *Backdraft* presentation, explanations of behind-the-scenes technology at *The World of Cinemagic*, and a cute cycle ride with *E.T.*

HIGHLIGHTS

- *Backdraft*
- *Backlot tram tour*
- *Back to The Future—The Ride*
- *Beethoven's Animal Actors Stage*
- *The Flintstones Show*
- *Jurassic Park—The Ride*
- *Marvel Mania restaurant*
- *Totally Nickelodeon*
- *WaterWorld show*
- *The Wild, Wild, Wild West Stunt Show*
- *The World of Cinemagic*

INFORMATION

✚	Inside front cover
✉	Universal City Drive (off I–101/Hollywood Freeway)
☎	818/622–3801
◷	Summer daily 8AM–10PM (box office 7–5); winter daily 9–7 (box office 8:30–4). Closed Thanksgiving, Christmas
🍴	Wide range of dining and fast-food options (S–SS)
▭	420, 424, 425, 522
♿	Good
💲	Very expensive (tickets include admission to rides, shows, and attractions); children under 3 free. Parking: moderate
↔	Griffith Park (➤ 32)
❓	Regularly scheduled Spanish- and Japanese-language tram tours. French-language tours can be booked ahead

GRIFFITH PARK

A vast open-air playground straddling the Hollywood hills, Griffith Park offers a raft of sights and activities, the Autry Museum (▶ 33), and, from its landmark copper-domed Observatory, the best view of the Hollywood sign.

A handsome bequest The largest municipal park in the United States, Griffith Park lies in the foothills of the Santa Monica Mountains. The original 3,015-acre site was given to the city in 1896 by Col. Griffith Jenkins Griffith, who also left a trust with sufficient funds to build the amphitheater-style Greek Theatre, a favorite outdoor concert venue, and the Griffith Observatory, which overlooks the city and houses an astronomy museum. There are daily planetarium and laserium shows, and on clear evenings you can inspect the heavens through a giant Zeiss telescope.

Around the park The huge park offers a tremendous variety of scenery. You can walk the cool, leafy Ferndell trail or reach the rugged high chaparral by a network of trails and easy-to-follow fire roads (maps from the Ranger Station). In the southeast corner of the park, near the Los Feliz exit, there are miniature train rides and children's pony rides. The antique merry-go-round, near the single, centrally located Ranger Station, is beloved of small children, and there are picnic areas, 28 tennis courts, and four golf courses (▶ 83) with plenty of parking near by. Further north, the Los Angeles Zoo offers 77 landscaped acres of animals and shows. Northwest, off Zoo Drive, the Los Angeles Equestrian Center rents out American quarter horses. The park's one Ranger Station can also supply a list of stables in the park area, including Sunset Ranch, which offers escorted moonlight rides ☎ 323/464 9612.

DID YOU KNOW?

- Size: 4,107 acres
- Elevation: between 384 and 1,625 feet above sea level
- The Observatory starred in the 1955 movie *Rebel Without a Cause*
- Santana, Johnny Mathis, and other acts selling over 100,000 tickets are commemorated in the Greek Theatre's Wall of Fame

INFORMATION

- ✚ Inside front cover
- ✉ Off I–5/Golden State Freeway and 134/Ventura Freeway in the north
- ☎ Ranger Station: 323/913–4688. Griffith Park Observatory: 323/664–1191. Laserium Concerts 818/997–3624. Los Angeles Equestrian Center: 818/840–9063. Los Angeles Zoo: 323/666–4650
- ◷ Daily 6–10 (trails and mountain roads close at sunset). Merry-Go-Round: weekends 11–5; daily in summer. Miniature train rides: daily 10–5. Pony rides: Tue–Sun 10–5
- 🍴 Refreshment stands (S)
- 🚌 96, 180, 181
- ♿ Good to nonexistent
- 🎫 Park entry and observatory: free. Fees for some other attractions and shows
- ↔ Autry Museum of Western Heritage (▶ 33)

10

AUTRY MUSEUM OF WESTERN HERITAGE

It's hard to walk away from this spirited and entertaining celebration of all things Western without coveting a Stetson or a bandanna. The seven galleries provide a riveting insight into American Western history and heritage.

The singing cowboy Housed in a California Mission-style complex, the museum is named for Gene Autry, singing cowboy of Hollywood Westerns and early TV fame. The Autry Foundation was a prime mover in the establishment of the museum, which tells the story of the West through its magnificent collections of Western art and artifacts—over 40,000 individual pieces.

Winning the West The wagon-train era exhibit is enlivened by recorded extracts from pioneer diaries and Indian artifacts, and real gold nuggets add a frisson of authenticity to tales of the California Gold Rush. The Spirit of the Community gallery explores European, Mexican, and Chinese migration in the Old West with lifestyle displays illustrating customs, costumes, and crafts. The Cowboy Gallery, full of all sorts of cowboy accoutrements, introduces famous gunslingers—and the guns they slung— plus the Spanish *vaqueros* who were herding cattle on horseback for 300 years before Mexican *charros*, the cowboys of popular imagery. Kids dress up in boots and spurs in the Children's Discovery Gallery. Upstairs, the Spirit of Imagination Gallery takes an intelligent look at Western culture as portrayed on screen.

HIGHLIGHTS

- Colt Firearms Collection
- Early art from the West
- Frederick Remington's bronze statues
- Indian beadwork and folk crafts
- Listening to recorded readings from pioneer diaries
- Trails West environmental display
- Western film and television memorabilia

INFORMATION

- ✚ Inside front cover
- ✉ 4700 Western Heritage Way, Griffith Park (junction of I–5/Golden State Freeway and 134/Ventura Freeway)
- ☎ 323/667–2000
- ◷ Tue–Sun 10–5. Closed Mon, Thanksgiving, Christmas
- 🍴 Golden Spur Café (S–SS)
- ▣ 96
- ♿ Excellent
- 💲 Moderate
- ↔ Universal Studios (▶ 31) Griffith Park (▶ 32)
- ❓ Frequent special exhibitions

HOLLYHOCK HOUSE

Set on a green mound in the Hollywood flatlands with views across the city, Frank Lloyd Wright's Hollyhock House is not only one of LA's most prestigious architectural treasures, but also a great place for a picnic.

DID YOU KNOW?

- Wright doubled the original budget of $25,000
- The Hollyhock House was gifted to the City in 1927
- Wright's son, Lloyd, oversaw renovations in the 1940s and 1970s
- The only original piece of leaded glass is a skylight
- The dining table and chairs are Wright originals; the sitting room furnishings are reproductions

INFORMATION

- ✚ H2
- ✉ Barnsdall Park, 4808 Hollywood Boulevard, Hollywood
- ☎ 323/913–4157
- ⊙ Wed–Sun tours at noon, 1, 2, 3. Closed Mon–Tue
- 🚌 1, 217
- ♿ None
- 💲 Inexpensive

Olive Hill Oil heiress and independent spirit Aline Barnsdall originally commissioned Wright to design a full-scale arts complex, incorporating a cinema, theater, studio-workshops and living quarters, on Olive Hill. Work began in 1917, but financial and artistic differences brought the project to an end in 1921 with only three buildings completed.

"Organic" design Planned as a home for Barnsdall and her young daughter, Hollyhock House crowns the crest of the hill and is named for Barnsdall's favorite flower. Hollyhocks appear in abstract form in the dramatic Maya-style geometric reliefs and pinnacles that adorn the squat concrete building. Part temple, part California Bungalow, Wright's "organic" design deliberately connects each significant interior space with its neighbor and with a related exterior space so clear progressive sight lines are established, and a sense of light and air predominates. The spatial complexity of the interior, with its raised and lowered floor and ceiling levels, contrasts with the relaxing autumnal color scheme and the simplicity of the materials—cement and wood. The wonderful roofscape was designed as an integral extension of the living space.

Design dictator Wright employed several cunning devices to ensure his vision of uncluttered space was adhered to. Canted walls prevented pictures being hung in the bedrooms, and extra wide baseboards meant no furniture could be placed against the walls.

NATURAL HISTORY MUSEUM

This is a truly enjoyable and imaginatively designed natural history museum, and there is far more to be seen than the usual array of stuffed birds, beasts, and prehistoric relatives.

The broad picture The museum's home is a handsome Spanish Renaissance Revival affair on the north side of Exposition Park. Its collections cover an enormous range of topics. In addition to the natural history exhibits there are superb Mesoamerican artifacts including gold jewelry and pottery from the Maya, Inca, and Aztec cultures; an excellent Native American Indian section with a re-created pueblo, intricate Plains Indian beadwork, and Navajo textiles; and California and American history galleries.

Natural wonders Much to the delight of *Jurassic Park* fans, the County Museum is big on fossils and dinosaurs. This is the place to ogle a *Sauropod*, a pin-headed 72-foot-long giant and one of the largest dinosaurs ever discovered. It probably weighed around 30–40 tons, dwarfing *Tyrannosaurus rex* (a mere 50 feet long and 6–7 tons). *Carnotaurus*, the meat-eating monster first discovered in Patagonia in 1984, also puts in an appearance, as does the rhino-like *Brontops*, or "Thunderbeast." The giant dioramas of African and North American mammals are terrific; and, on the geological front, there is a glittering Hall of Gems and Minerals. Do not miss the brilliant Discovery Center. Children love the imaginative touchy-feely games and toys, fossil rubbings, and other hands-on diversions. On the mezzanine level, the Insect Zoo offers a suitably creepy-crawly collection of slumbering scorpions, huge hissing cockroaches from Madagascar, pink-toed tarantulas, and nauseating assassin bugs.

DID YOU KNOW?

- The total weight of a swarm of African locusts: 300 million pounds (1,500 tons)
- The Jurassic fish with teeth longer than a great white shark: *Xiphactonus audax*
- The world's deepest natural diver: Emperor penguin (840 feet)
- World's fastest diver: peregrine falcon (180mph)
- The famous US prison named for a bird: Alcatraz (Spanish for pelican)
- The two biggest bird stars of jungle movie soundtracks: the Australian kookaburra and Indian blue peafowl

INFORMATION

- ✚ J11
- ✉ 900 Exposition Boulevard
- ☎ 213/744-3414
- ◕ Museum: Tue–Sun 10–5. Discovery Center: Tue–Fri 10–3; Sat–Sun 10–4. Closed Mon (except museum on national holidays), Thanksgiving, Christmas, New Year's Day
- 🍴 Cafeteria ($)
- 🚌 40, 42, 81; DASH C/Expo Park
- ♿ Very good
- 💰 Moderate
- ↔ Exposition Park Rose Garden (▶ 57)

35

WELLS FARGO HISTORY MUSEUM

DID YOU KNOW?

- Average speed of a Concord Stagecoach: 5mph
- Number of horses: 6 (changed every 12 miles)
- Duration of journey from Omaha to Sacramento: 15 days
- Cost: $300
- Baggage limit: 25lb per person
- Pony Express: operational April 1860 to October 1861
- Original route (duration): St. Joseph, MO, to Sacramento, CA (1,966 miles in 10–12 days)
- Total mail carried: 35,000 letters

INFORMATION

- ➕ M7
- ✉ 333 S Grand Avenue
- ☎ 213/253–7166
- 🕐 Mon–Fri 9–5. Closed Sat–Sun
- 🚌 DASH B
- ♿ Good
- 🎫 Free
- ↔ Museum of Contemporary Art (➤ 37)
  Grand Central Market (➤ 38)
  California Plaza (➤ 54)
  Biltmore Hotel (➤ 56)
  Los Angeles Central Library (➤ 56)

An Old West legend right up there with the Colt Six-Shooter, Wyatt Earp and Buffalo Bill Cody, Wells Fargo celebrates the company's rip-roaring early history with tales of the Forty-Niners, the Pony Express, and Concord Stagecoaches.

Expanding west By 1852, when Henry Wells and William G. Fargo set up their Western banking and express service in San Francisco, the California Gold Rush was in full swing. The new venture swiftly established a reputation for buying, selling, and transporting gold and valuables. In the early 1860s, Wells, Fargo & Co took over the western leg of the famed Pony Express. They operated a stagecoach service from the 1860s, and were among the first to take to the rails when the transcontinental railroad was completed in 1869.

"Cradle on Wheels" Centerstage in the museum goes to an original Concord Stagecoach, named for its birthplace in Concord, Mass. Though Mark Twain romantically described it as a "cradle on wheels," the reality of a stagecoach journey was far from relaxing. Up to 18 passengers, including the driver and guard, could be squeezed into the nine-seat leather upholstered interior and on to the open-air upper deck. Stops were infrequent, the food barely edible, and aside from the constant jolting, dust, and discomfort, perils of the road included highwaymen and frequent accidents. Among the other artifacts on display, there is no missing the plum-sized gold nugget found in California's Feather River, near Challenge, in 1975. This lucky find weighed in at 26.4oz. Another eye-catcher is a 7,500lb, 19th-century safe handpainted with tranquil pastoral scenes and flowers, supposed to allay customers' concerns.

MUSEUM OF CONTEMPORARY ART

A single museum with two addresses a mile apart, MOCA has a growing catalogue of post-1940 artworks that constitutes one of the most important contemporary art collections in the United States.

Downtown All blonde wood and vast white spaces, MOCA's Downtown galleries, designed by Japanese architect Arata Isozaki, present a frequently changing program of both shows drawn from the extensive permanent collection and touring exhibitions. The busy calendar also introduces newly commissioned projects and works by established and emerging artists in a broad variety of media.

Across town While Isozaki's museum was under construction, MOCA transformed a spacious warehouse in Little Tokyo into gallery space, now known as the Geffen Contemporary at MOCA. The vast industrial space, with its ramps and girders, is ideal for big installation pieces. Smaller works occupy a maze of galleries overlooked from a mezzanine level. In an interesting display designed to provide a loose comparative time-frame for contemporary art, a series of four "context rooms" notes major historical, political, and artistic developments since the 1940s.

HIGHLIGHTS

Works by:
- De Kooning
- Giacometti
- Mondrian
- Pollock
- Oldenburg

INFORMATION

MOCA
- ✚ M7
- ✉ 250 S Grand Avenue
- ☎ 213/626–6222
- ◉ Tue–Sun 11–5 (Thu until 8). Closed Mon, Thanksgiving, Christmas, New Year's Day
- ⅋ Patinette at MOCA (S–SS)
- ▣ DASH B
- ♿ Good
- ⊡ Moderate (includes both buildings); free on Thu after 5
- ⟷ Wells Fargo History Museum (▶ 36)
  California Plaza (▶ 54)
  Biltmore Hotel (▶ 56)
  Los Angeles Central Library (▶ 56)
- ❓ Regularly scheduled art talks program, free with museum admission
  ☎ 213/621–1757

Geffen Contemporary
- ✚ N7
- ✉ 152 N Central Avenue
- ▣ DASH A
- ⟷ Little Tokyo (▶ 40)
  Japanese American National Museum (▶ 50)

15

GRAND CENTRAL MARKET

DID YOU KNOW?

- *Chiles rellenos*: stuffed sweet peppers, usually filled with meat and rice
- *Chipotle*: smoked jalapeño pepper with a sweet taste
- *Churros*: deep-fried pastry
- *Criadillas*: bull's testicles
- *Gorditas*: fried corn and potato pockets filled with meat and beans
- *Tamales*: corn dough parcels filled with chicken or meat, or with almonds and raisins

INFORMATION

- M7
- 317 S Broadway
- 213/624–2378
- Mon–Sat 9–6; Sun 10–5
- Several Mexican fast-food takeout stalls, Chinese noodle café, and a juice bar (all S)
- Civic Center
- DASH D
- Angel's Flight
- None
- Free
- Wells Fargo History Museum (➤ 36)
  Museum of Contemporary Art (➤ 37)
  Bradbury Building (➤ 39)
  California Plaza (➤ 54)
  Biltmore Hotel (➤ 56)

For anyone who loves food or markets, Downtown's colorful produce market is a real find. In addition to providing a feast for the eyes, it is also a great place to grab picnic food or stop for a snack.

Downtown's historic larder LA's largest and oldest food market, a maze of closely packed stalls, first opened its doors in 1917, and the hangar-like building, with entrances on both Broadway and Hill Street, has been feeding the Downtown district ever since. In those days, Broadway was LA's poshest thoroughfare, while today it is the heart of the city's crowded Hispanic shopping district. The market steps up several gears from busy to seething on Saturdays when the noise and the bustle is unbelievable.

Capsicums and cacti There is sawdust on the floor and butchers' knives chop-chop and thud away on a dozen counters. Capsicums, avocados, and big beefy tomatoes are stacked into glossy piles alongside stalks of celery, potatoes in myriad hues, huge bunches of bananas, and pyramids of oranges, lemons, limes, and apples. Among the less familiar offerings are prickly pears, cactus leaves, and dozens of different types of fresh and dried chillies available in varying degrees of ferocity. Meanwhile, the Mexican butchers display bits of beasts one would rather not even think about—vegetarians will want to avoid this area. There are more than 50 stalls in all, including fish merchants and bakers, confectioners, delicatessens selling cheese and cold meats, spice merchants, dried fruit and nut sellers, and the Chinese herbal medicine man. Takeout food stalls do a roaring trade in Mexican snacks, and there are quick-bite stops with tables and chairs near the Hill Street exit.

BRADBURY BUILDING

The Bradbury, just across the street from the Grand Central Market, is a hidden treasure. It is architecturally one-of-a-kind, and its bizarre history is intriguing.

A millionaire's monument In 1892 elderly and ailing mining millionaire Lewis Bradbury turned down the plans of respected local architect Sumner Hunt for a splendid five-story building he wished to construct as a monument to his achievements. Instead, for no explicable reason, he invited an obscure architect's draftsman, 32-year-old George Wyman, to submit designs. Wyman initially refused, but one evening as he sat at a ouija-board with his wife, they received a message from his dead brother, which read "Take the Bradbury building. It will make you famous." Spurred on by this occult communication, and inspired by Edward Bellamy's 1887 science fiction novel *Looking Backward*, which actually looked forward to life in a Utopian society in the year 2000, Wyman created a dazzling futuristic building that ranks among the marvels of the age.

From fiction to fact The Bradbury's Italianate façade is attractive but unexceptional. However, the soaring, light-filled atrium is amazing. Light pours down through the narrow well, drawing the eye immediately upward and dramatizing the sensation of height. Against a backdrop of golden-yellow Mexican tiles, pink glazed brick, and polished oak, intricate, black wrought-iron railings edge the balconies and flights of marble steps climb five stories to the roof. Though Wyman took a correspondence course in architecture after he completed the Bradbury, he never designed another significant building. Unfortunately Lewis Bradbury died just before his monument was opened in 1893.

DID YOU KNOW?

- Wyman imported Belgian marble for the staircases, and the French wrought-iron decorations were displayed at the 1893 Chicago World Fair before being installed
- The building cost Bradbury $500,000, more than three times the initial estimates
- A popular movie location, the Bradbury appeared in *DOA* (1949), *Good Neighbor Sam* (1964), *Blade Runner* (1982), *Last Action Hero* (1993), and *Murder in the First* (1994)

INFORMATION

- ✛ M7
- ✉ 304 S Broadway (access to the hallway only)
- ☎ 213/626–1893
- 🕐 Mon–Sat 9–5. Closed Sun
- 🚇 Civic Center
- 🚌 DASH D
- ♿ None
- 💲 Free
- 🔗 Wells Fargo History Museum (➤ 36)
  Museum of Contemporary Art (➤ 37)
  Grand Central Market (➤ 38)
  California Plaza (➤ 54)
  Biltmore Hotel (➤ 56)

LITTLE TOKYO

The hub of LA's 200,000-strong Japanese-American community, Little Tokyo is pleasantly low-key and walkable. There are surprise outposts of Japanese landscaping tucked into the concrete jungle, and plenty of craft shops to nose around.

Historical footnotes Bounded by 1st and 3rd, Los Angeles and San Pedro streets, this area was first settled at the end of the 19th century. Several historic buildings remain on 1st Street, which leads down to the Japanese American National Museum (➤ 50).

Sushi **and** ***shiatsu*** Over the road, among the neat green pompoms of pollarded trees and bright blue tile roofs, Japanese Village Plaza's 40 restaurants and small shops, exotic supermarkets, *sushi* bars, and *shiatsu* massage parlors make for interesting browsing. Cross 2nd Street for the Japanese-American Cultural and Community Center, where the Doizaki Gallery exhibits Japanese artworks. The adjacent Japan America Theater presents contemporary and traditional Japanese performances such as Noh plays and Kabuki theater productions. Outside, on Noguchi Plaza, a huge stone memorial commemorates the *Issei* (first generation Japanese-Americans).

Garden oasis Another feature of the plaza is the delightful James Irvine Garden, a Japanese-style oasis encircled by a stream, with paths, bridges, stepping stones, trees, and flowering shrubs such as azaleas. There is more elegant Japanese landscaping near by, outside the Higashi Hongwanji Buddhist Temple 505 E 3rd Street, where dwarf pines, grassy tuffets, and rock arrangements front the graceful neotraditional façade.

EL PUEBLO DE LOS ANGELES

This historic area, officially a city park, is a a favorite with visitors. Angelenos tend to be snooty about the touristy Olvera Street market, but Sunday's mariachi *masses in the Old Plaza Church are worthwhile, as are the more conventional historic sights.*

LA's historic heart Wedged between Chinatown and Downtown, the site of the original 1781 pueblo settlement covers just a handful of city blocks. Within its confines are 27 historic buildings, including two museums, restaurants, shops, and a Mexican street market. The main thoroughfare is pedestrianized Olvera Street, leading off La Placita, the former town plaza shaded by Moreton Bay fig trees. On the south side of the plaza, free guided walking tours ☺ Tue–Sat 10, 11, noon, 1 leave from a low brick building alongside the original 1884 Firehouse No. 1, which displays antique firefighting equipment. The Old Plaza Church, on the west side, is the city's oldest Catholic church, dedicated in 1822.

Sterling support One of the oldest streets in the city, Olvera Street fell into disrepair around the turn of the century when the Downtown area moved south. By 1926, it was a grimy, mud-filled alley until local civic leader Christine Sterling stepped in. The story of Sterling's campaign to rescue the historic buildings and inaugurate the market in the 1930s is told in a display at the restored Avila Adobe.

Mexican marketplace Across the street, the Visitors Center in the 1887 Sepulveda House distributes walking tour maps, and shows a short video history of the city. The market is still going strong, and the crowded thoroughfare is bursting with dozens of stalls selling everything from Mexican pottery and leatherware to sombreros.

DID YOU KNOW?

- Original settlement: Pueblo de Nuestra Señora la Reina de los Angeles (Our Lady Queen of the Angels)
- Oldest existing building: Avila Adobe (1818)
- The adobe (mud) walls of the Avila House are 3 feet thick
- The Avila House served as headquarters for Commodore Robert Stockton of the US Army during the Mexican–American War
- The Moreton Bay fig trees on the plaza were planted in the 1870s

INFORMATION

Visitors Center
- ✚ N6
- ✉ W-12 Olvera Street
- ☎ 213/628–1274
- ☺ Mon–Sat 10–3. Closed Sun
- 🚇 DASH B, D
- ♿ Few
- 🎫 Free
- ↔ Chinatown (➤ 17) Union Station (➤ 56)
- ❓ Cinco de Mayo (May 5) and Dia de los Muertos (Nov 2) festivals (➤ 22)

Museums
- ☺ Avila Adobe: daily 10–4. Plaza Firehouse: Tue–Sun 10–3
- 🎫 Free

LONG BEACH AND THE *QUEEN MARY*

DID YOU KNOW?

The *Queen Mary*
- Launched: Clydeside, Scotland, September 26 1934
- Portholes: 2,000-plus
- Gross tonnage: 81,237
- Passengers/crew: 1,957/1,174
- No. of transatlantic crossings: 1,001

INFORMATION

Long Beach Area Convention & Visitors Bureau
- ✛ Inside front cover
- ✉ One World Trade Center, Ocean Boulevard
- ☎ 562/436–3645
- 🕐 Mon–Fri 8:30–5
- 🚇 Metro Blue Line/Pacific Avenue
- 🚌 60
- 🎫 Free

The *Queen Mary*
- ✉ Queen Mary Seaport, off I–710/Long Beach Freeway
- ☎ 310/435–3511
- 🕐 Daily 10–6
- ♿ Few
- 🎫 Expensive

Aquarium of the Pacific
- ✉ 310 Golden Shore
- ☎ 562/590–3100
- 🕐 Daily 10–6
- ♿ Very good
- 🎫 Moderate

An easy day trip south from central Los Angeles, Long Beach has plenty to offer visitors—from the regal **Queen** Mary *and a state-of-the-art aquarium to water-sports, shopping and gondola rides.*

On the water A convenient first stop at the foot of the freeway, the *Queen Mary* finally came to rest here in 1967. What was until recently the largest liner afloat is now a hotel, but regular guided tours give access to the engine rooms, cabin suites and gorgeous art deco salons. Across the Queensway Bay Bridge (water taxi service available), the excellent Aquarium of the Pacific showcases over 550 marine species from the northern Pacific to the tropics, including sharks, giant octopuses and California sea lions. East from here Shoreline Drive skirts San Pedro Bay , passing the Long Beach Arena encircled by the world's biggest mural, *Plant Ocean*, by the marine artist Wyland (like the artist formerly known as Prince, he sticks with a single name). Shoreline Village is popular for shopping and dining, with boat trips (➤ 19) and views of the *Queen Mary*.

Downtown to Venice Island Pine Avenue, at the heart of downtown Long Beach, bustles with shops and restaurants. Take Ocean Drive east to Belmont Shores, where concessionaires rent out water-sports equipment, and bikes and skates for riding the beach path. Behind the beach 2nd Street is home to a mixed bag of shops and restaurants, and crosses on to Naples Island. This affluent residential neighborhood, criss-crossed with canals, was developed in the 1920s. Explore it on foot, or take a ride with Gondola Getaway (➤ 19).

RANCHO LOS ALAMITOS

Set in lovely gardens, this historic ranch house, which grew up around the country's oldest domestic adobe (1806), brings a touch of the country to the heart of the city with its lovely gardens. There are house tours, a small farmyard full of animals, and on selected weekends cultural events.

Spanish land grant Now tucked away behind the gates of an exclusive residential development not far from Long Beach, the ranch house was once master of all it surveyed. The original 28,500-acre rancho was part of an enormous land grant allocated to a Spanish soldier, Manuel Nieto, in 1790. The Bixby family took possession of the property in 1881, and the house remained in the family for almost a century until it was donated to the City of Long Beach in 1968.

A family home The Bixbys were one of Southern California's most prominent pioneer ranching families, and Los Alamitos was the family home of Fred Bixby (1875–1952). From humble beginnings, the ranch house spread out on its hilltop site, and the views stretched across wheatfields to the ocean. During the 1920s and '30s, Fred's wife, Florence (1875–1961), set about developing the gardens, which are one of the highlights today. There is a distinctly Mexican-Mediterranean feel to the low white-washed walls and shaded walkways. Look for the lovely rose garden, an impressively spiky cacti collection and native Californian plantings. Tours of the house reveal that the original furnishings and family portraits are still in place. Five turn-of-the-century barns house a black-smith's shop, tackroom, and stables with Shire draft horses. Children enjoy the sheep and goats, ducks, chickens, rabbits, and doves.

DID YOU KNOW?

- The ranch occupies a hilltop 40 feet above sea level
- Gabrieleno Native Americans founded the village of Puvunga here in around AD 500
- Of Manuel Nieto's original 300,000-acre Spanish land grant, only 7.5 acres remain
- The first simple adobe shelter on this site was built around 1800
- The Moreton Bay fig on the property, its biggest tree, was planted in 1881

INFORMATION

- ✚ Inside back cover
- ✉ 6400 Bixby Hill Road (take 7th Street east; left on Studebaker Road; left on Anaheim)
- ☎ 562/431–3541
- 🕐 Wed–Sun 1–5 (last tour at 4)
- 🚌 LBT 42
- ♿ Few
- 💲 Free
- ↔ Long Beach and the *Queen Mary* (➤ 42)
- ❓ Call for information about events and monthly Sunday afternoon education programs (mostly free)

GAMBLE HOUSE

HIGHLIGHTS

- Front entrance: leaded glass by Emil Lange
- Main staircase
- Sitting room: carved reliefs of birds and plants
- Rugs from Greene and Greene designs
- Dining room furniture
- Tricks of the butler's pantry such as rollers for storing ironed tablecloths so that creases were never folded in to mar their perfection
- Guest bedroom: maple furnishings inlaid with silver

INFORMATION

- Inside back cover
- 4 Westmoreland Place, Pasadena (off N Orange Grove, just south of Rosemont)
- 626/793–3334
- Thu–Sun noon–3. Closed Mon–Wed and holidays
- 177, 267
- None
- Inexpensive
- Old Pasadena (➤ 18) Norton Simon Museum of Art (➤ 45) Huntington Library, Art Collections and Botanical Gardens (➤ 46) Los Angeles State and County Arboretum (➤ 47) Descanso Gardens (➤ 57)
- Admission by guided tour only; frequent departures

The Gamble House takes the utilitarian California Bungalow and turns it into an art form. Every impeccably handcrafted inch of this superb American Arts and Crafts Movement house is a masterpiece.

The California Bungalow The Gamble House, designed by the architect brothers Charles and Henry Greene for David and Mary Gamble (of Procter and Gamble fame), is the most complete and well-preserved example of a handful of luxurious wooden "bungalows" built in the first decade of the 20th century. The informal bungalow-style residence represented an appealing escape from Victorian stuffiness, and it was swiftly translated into Southern California's architectural vernacular.

A symphony in wood The Gamble House is, however, far from being a traditional bungalow. Greene and Greene's spreading two-story design, with its Japanese-influenced lines, was planned in meticulous detail. The site was chosen to catch cool breezes from the Arroyo, and the arrangement of spacious verandas shaded by second-story sleeping porches and overhanging eaves keeps the house comfortably ventilated. Working largely in wood, the Greenes cloaked the exterior with shingles and created a rich, golden timbered interior using Burmese teak, oak, maple, redwood, and cedar. Every fixture and fitting, from the dining room furniture to the andirons in the fireplace, was custom-built, and many of the schemes were designed to complement Mary Gamble's favorite possessions such as Tiffany table lamps and opalescent Rockwood pottery. Architectural students and enthusiasts should not miss the excellent bookstore, which also sells self-guided map tours around other Pasadena historic homes.

NORTON SIMON MUSEUM OF ART

If you have time to visit only one art museum in Los Angeles, make it the Norton Simon. Though the collections gathered here are less well known than those of the Getty Center (▶ 25) or LACMA (▶ 28), their range and quality are in many ways superior to both.

Industrialist and collector The collections were originally founded as the Pasadena Art Institute in 1924. From the 1960s, under the direction of wealthy industrialist and collector Norton Simon (1907–1993), the museum has grown into a world-class collection of European Old Master, Impressionist and Post-Impressionist works, as well as Asian sculpture, arranged in galleries around a lawned sculpture garden.

The collections The collections begin with jewel-like 14th-century Italian religious paintings and Renaissance art. The ravishing *Branchini Madonna* is just one of the highlights; the collection includes works by Filippino Lippi, Botticelli, Bellini, and Cranach. From the 17th and 18th centuries there are Rembrandt portraits; Canaletto's minutely detailed Venetian scenes drawn with a master draftsman's skill; soft, plump Tiepolo figures; and Rubens's oils on a heroic scale. The superb 19th- to 20th-century galleries boast major works by Monet, Renoir, Cézanne, and Van Gogh, and a fistful of color from Matisse, Kandinsky, Braque, and Klee. The superb Degas Collection numbers more than 100 pieces, including rare landscapes, enigmatic monotypes, and an exceptional series of bronze dancers posthumously cast from wax models found in the artist's studio. The museum also possesses a rich collection of Hindu and Buddhist sculpture from Nepal, India, Thailand, and Cambodia.

HIGHLIGHTS

- *Branchini Madonna,* Giovanni di Paolo
- *Presumed Portrait of the Artist's Son, Titus,* Rembrandt
- *Burghers of Calais,* Rodin
- *The Stonebreakers,* Seurat
- *Exotic Landscape,* Rousseau
- *Flower Vendor,* Rivera
- *Odalisque with Tambourine,* Matisse
- *Woman with Book,* Picasso
- Degas Collection
- *The Mulberry Tree,* Van Gogh (below)

INFORMATION

- Inside back cover
- 411 W Colorado Boulevard, Pasadena
- 626/449–6840
- Thu–Sun noon–6. Closed Mon–Wed
- 177, 180, 181
- Good
- Inexpensive
- Old Pasadena (▶ 18)

23

THE HUNTINGTON

INFORMATION

- Inside back cover
- 1151 Oxford Road, San Marino (Pasadena)
- 626/405–2141
- Sep–May Tue–Fri 12–4:30. Sat–Sun 10:30–4:30. Jun–Aug Tue–Sun 10:30–4:30. Closed Mon and major holidays
- Restaurant and tea room (S–SS)
- 79, 379
- Good
- Moderate; free first Thu of month
- Old Pasadena (► 18) Gamble House (► 44) Norton Simon Museum of Art (► 45) Los Angeles State and County Arboretum (► 47)
- Garden tours daily at 1

Above: Sarah Siddons as the Tragic Muse, *Sir Joshua Reynolds*

Three separate elements—manuscripts, paintings, and the gardens—contribute to the famously rich and varied Huntington experience, and there hardly seems enough time to do each of them justice.

Railroad tycoon Henry E. Huntington (1850–1927) moved to LA in 1902 and made a second fortune organizing the city's rail system. When he retired to devote himself to his library, he married his uncle's widow, Arabella, who shared his interest in art. Together they amassed the core collections of 18th-century British portraits and French furnishings and decorative arts, setting up a trust bequeathing them for public benefit in 1919.

Manuscripts The Library building's extraordinary treasury of rare and precious manuscripts and books spans 800 years, from the famous 13th-century Ellesmere Chaucer to handwritten drafts of novels and poems by, for example, William Blake, Walt Whitman, and Jack London.

Fine art The 1910 Beaux-Arts mansion, by Myron Hunt and Elmer Grey, displays the famous portrait collection, including Gainsborough's *Blue Boy*. Here too you will find ornate French furnishings and porcelain, and 18th-century European paintings added since Huntington's day. The Virginia Steele Scott Gallery houses recent acquisitions of American art from the 18th to early 20th centuries, and furnishings from the Arts and Crafts Movement team Greene and Greene (► 44).

Glorious gardens Huntington began work on the spectacular 130-acre gardens in collaboration with William Hertrich in 1904. Today, there are 14,000 types of plants and trees in 15 separate garden areas. The camellia woods are at their peak in spring, the rose garden in summer.

LA STATE & COUNTY ARBORETUM

Set against the backdrop of the San Gabriel Mountains, these lovely gardens in a corner of the old Rancho Santa Anita offer year-round color and interest. They are also a great place to unwind.

Mexican rancho Rancho Santa Anita was one of several ranches in the valley when Hugo Reid built his adobe house here in 1839. Furnished in simple pioneer style, it is one of three historic buildings in the grounds. The others are silver mining millionaire E.J. "Lucky" Baldwin's fairy-tale 1881 guesthouse, and the 1890 Santa Anita Railroad Depot.

From *Acacia* to *Ziziphus* The lush profusion of trees and plants (the arboretum is a favorite exotic movie location) includes exuberant jungle areas, towering palms, splashing water-falls, and quiet corners to enjoy the peace—as long as the raucous peacocks are silent. Seek out the aquatic garden, the tropical greenhouse, the demonstration home gardens, and the California landscape area, which shows the valley's natural state. There is much to see, so consider taking a tram tour to the further reaches of the grounds.

DID YOU KNOW?

- 36,000 plants from 5,000 species grow in the gardens
- 15,000-plus handmade bricks were used to construct the Hugo Reid Adobe, a California Historic Landmark
- 25 different types of palm tree grow in LA. The most common is the Mexican fan palm, the rarest *Jabaeopsis Caffra*, grown in the arboretum
- Scenes for the Humphrey Bogart–Katharine Hepburn movie *The African Queen* (1951) were filmed in the tropical gardens

INFORMATION

- ✛ Inside back cover
- ✉ 301 N Baldwin Road, Arcadia (off I–210/Foothill Freeway)
- ☎ 626/821–3222
- ◷ Daily 9–5 (last ticket sales 4:30). Closed Christmas
- 🍴 Coffee shop (S)
- 🚌 78, 79, 268
- ♿ Few
- 💲 Inexpensive
- ⇄ Old Pasadena (▶ 18)
  Gamble House (▶ 44)
  Norton Simon Museum of Art (▶ 45)
  Huntington Library, Art Collections and Botanical Gardens (▶ 46)
- ❓ Regular tram tours visit the extensive grounds

DISNEYLAND

HIGHLIGHTS

- Jungle Cruise (Adventureland)
- Big Thunder Mountain Railroad (Frontierland)
- Honey, I Shrunk the Audience (Tomorrowland)
- Pirates of the Caribbean (New Orleans Square)
- Splash Mountain (Critter Country)
- Star Tours (Tomorrowland)

INFORMATION

- Inside back cover
- 1313 Harbor Boulevard (off I–5/Santa Ana Freeway), Anaheim
- 714/781–4565
- Daily. Call for schedules. Approximate hours peak season 9AM–midnight or 1AM. Low season Mon–Fri 10–6; Sat 9–midnight; Sun 9–10
- Snack bars, cafés, and restaurants ($–$$$)
- 460
- Excellent
- Very expensive (all rides and shows inclusive)
- Call ahead for details of nighttime shows and special holiday events

Since Disneyland opened its doors in 1955, Disney theme parks have become a world-wide phenomenon. The 80 acres that started it all offer a beguiling combination of more than 60 shows and attractions, plus appearances by favorite Disney cartoon characters. Even if you've seen other Disney parks, don't miss the original.

Magic Kingdom Brilliantly conceived and operated like Swiss clockwork, Disney's particular brand of fantasy appeals across almost all age and cultural barriers. The park is divided into eight individually themed "lands." The gates open on to Main Street USA, a pastiche Victorian street lined with stores, which leads to the hub of the park at Sleeping Beauty Castle. From here you can explore the tropically inspired Adventureland, home to the rattling roller-coaster ride Indiana Jones™ Adventure, or take a turn around Wild West-style Frontierland. Small children favor the simpler, often-cartoonlike rides in Fantasyland and Mickey's Toontown, while New Orleans Square has the ultra-spooky Haunted Mansion. Tomorrowland, now a vision of the future as seen in the past, stars mini space-ships and planet models, Rocket Rods XPR (Disneyland's fastest and longest ride to date), and the perennially popular Space Mountain all-in-the-dark rollercoaster.

Think ahead Getting the best out of Disneyland calls for advance planning. From July to early September, and in holiday periods, the park is very crowded and lines can be long. Weekends are especially busy (Sundays tend to be better than Saturdays). Arrive early (the ticket office opens 30 minutes before the park) and make a dash for the best rides (► above and Highlights).

Top: Sleeping Beauty Castle

LOS ANGELES'
best

MUSEUMS

La Brea tar pits

Oozing from a fissure in the earth's crust, these gooey black tar pits are one of the world's most famous fossil sites. For thousands of years plants, birds, and animals have been trapped and entombed here, turning the asphalt into a paleontological soup from which scientists have recovered millions of fossilized remnants from some 420 species of animal and 140 types of plant. Most of the fossils date from 10,000 to 40,000 years ago.

BANNING RESIDENCE MUSEUM
Entrepreneur and "father of Los Angeles transportation," Phineas Banning (1830–1885) built this grand Greek Revival mansion in 1864. Splendid Colonial furnishings, a 19th-century carriage barn, and a park for picnicking.
🚹 Off map, south ✉ 401 East M Street, Wilmington (off I–110/Harbor Freeway) ☎ 310/548–7777 🕐 Tue–Thu 12:30–2:30; Sat–Sun 12:30–3:30. Closed Mon, Fri. Tours every hour 🚌 232 ♿ None 💲 Inexpensive

CALIFORNIA SCIENCE CENTER
Dozens of hands-on science, technology, and environmental displays designed to appeal to children, plus an IMAX theater.
🚹 J11 ✉ 700 State Drive, Exposition Park ☎ 213/744–7400 🕐 Daily 10–5. Call for IMAX schedules 🚌 DASH F/Expo Park ♿ Very good 💲 Free (except IMAX theater)

GEORGE C. PAGE MUSEUM OF LA BREA DISCOVERIES
Built with children in mind, this fascinating museum displays fossilized finds from the La Brea tar pits including a 12-foot-tall Imperial Mammoth skeleton (➤ panel for details).
🚹 Off map, west ✉ 5801 Wilshire Boulevard, Midtown ☎ 323/936–2230 🕐 Tue–Sun 10–5 🚌 20, 21, 22, 217, 320 ♿ Good 💲 Moderate

JAPANESE AMERICAN NATIONAL MUSEUM
The story of Japanese migration to the US, and the Japanese-Americans' struggle for acceptance in their adopted home.

The splendid glass dome of the Natural History Museum of Los Angeles County

Particularly moving exhibits deal with the World War II isolation camps.

➕ N7 ✉ 369 E 1st Street ☎ 213/625–0414 🕐 Tue–Sun 10–5; Thu until 8 🚌 DASH A ♿ Good 💲 Inexpensive

LOS ANGELES MARITIME MUSEUM

The largest maritime museum on the Pacific coast overlooks the busy Port of Los Angeles. In addition to dozens of beautifully crafted model ships, art, and seafaring artifacts, there are real ships to visit.

➕ Off map, south ✉ Berth 84 (end of 6th Street), San Pedro ☎ 310/548–7618 🕐 Tue–Sun 10–5 🚌 447 ♿ Good 💲 Inexpensive

MUSEUM OF NEON ART

This one-of-a-kind museum displays vintage and contemporary neon signs and sculptures, and offers monthly nighttime tours of LA's finest neon.

➕ L8 ✉ 501 W Olympic Boulevard ☎ 213/489–9918 🕐 Tue–Sun 11–6; Thu until 8 🚌 DASH C, E ♿ Few 💲 Inexpensive

Mona, by Lili Lakich, in the Museum of Neon Art

MUSEUM OF TELEVISION AND RADIO

This tribute to more than 70 years of home entertainment investigates aspects of broadcasting from news to *Star Trek* make-up.

➕ Off map, west ✉ 465 N Beverly Drive, Beverly Hills ☎ 310/786–1000 🕐 Wed–Sun noon–5; Thu until 9 🚌 3, 4 ♿ Good 💲 Moderate

MUSEUM OF TOLERANCE

The Simon Wiesenthal Center's thought-provoking museum explores the nature of prejudice (► panel for details).

➕ Off map, west ✉ 9786 W Pico Boulevard, West LA ☎ 310/553–8403 🕐 Mon–Thu 10–4; Fri 10–3 (Nov–Mar until 1PM); Sun 11–4 🚌 SM7 ♿ Very good 💲 Moderate

PACIFIC ASIA MUSEUM

Notable Far Eastern art is displayed in rotation alongside visiting exhibitions in an exotic 1920s interpretation of a Chinese imperial palace.

➕ Off map, northeast ✉ 46 N Los Robles Avenue, Pasadena ☎ 626/449–2742 🕐 Wed–Sun 10–5 🚌 180, 181, 188, 256, 260, 401 ♿ Few 💲 Inexpensive

SOUTHWEST MUSEUM

One of the finest collections of Native American art and artifacts in the country; pity about the somewhat lackluster displays.

➕ Off map, north ✉ 234 Museum Road (Avenue 43 exit off I-110/Pasadena Freeway) ☎ 323/221–2164 🕐 Tue–Sun 11–5 🚌 81, 83 ♿ Few 💲 Inexpensive

Beit Hashoah (House of the Holocaust)

Opened in 1993, less than a year after the LA riots (► 12), the Museum of Tolerance focuses its attentions on both the dynamics of prejudice and racism in America, and the history of the Holocaust. High-tech interactive and experiential exhibits offer a challenging insight into the machinations of bigotry. World War II artifacts and documents on the second floor provide the most moving memorial of all.

TV & MOVIE BUFF STUFF

See Top 25 Sights for
HOLLYWOOD BOULEVARD (► 30)
UNIVERSAL STUDIOS (► 31)

Grave affair

For years a mysterious veiled lady in black brought flowers to Rudolph Valentino's vault at Hollywood Memorial Park Cemetery, 6000 Santa Monica Boulevard, Hollywood, on the anniversary of his death. Others come to visit Cecil B. De Mille, Tyrone Power, and Douglas Fairbanks Sr. Buster Keaton, Stan Laurel, and Bette Davis are among those buried at Forest Lawn Memorial Park, 6300 Forest Lawn Drive. Marilyn Monroe, Natalie Wood, and Roy Orbison are at Westwood Memorial Park, 1218 Glendon Avenue.

Forest Lawn Memorial Park

BROADWAY HISTORIC THEATER DISTRICT

For movie fans with an interest in the early days, Downtown Broadway is the place to find the fabulous movie palaces of yesteryear. Several, such as the Los Angeles (No. 615), the Palace (No. 630), and the Orpheum (► 56), are still open. Guided walk tours are available with the Los Angeles Conservancy (► 19).

➕ M7–8 ▨ Broadway, between 3rd and 9th Streets
🚇 Pershing Square 🚌 27, 28, 45, 46

ENTERTAINMENT INDUSTRY DEVELOPMENT CORPORATION

If you want to see moviemakers on location, pick up a free copy of the daily shoot sheet from the fifth-floor permit office. It lists every motion picture, television program, commercial, and video being shot in the streets of the city that day.

➕ D1 ▨ 7083 Hollywood Boulevard, Hollywood ☎ 323/957–1000
🕐 Mon–Fri 8–6 🚌 1, 217

FREDERICK'S OF HOLLYWOOD LINGERIE MUSEUM

This selection of star undergarments displays offerings from Marilyn Monroe, Ingrid Bergman, Zsa Zsa Gabor, Cher, and Joan Collins. Further examples of Frederick's creative way with the female form include the cleavage-enhancing Depth Charge bra.

➕ D1 ▨ 6608 Hollywood Boulevard, Hollywood ☎ 323/466–8506
🕐 Mon–Sat 10–6; Sun noon–5 🚌 1 ♿ None 💵 Free

GRAVE LINE TOURS
A two-and-a-half hour orgy of titillating trivia delivered on cue as passengers (known as "bodies") are chauffeur-driven (in a hearse) past the former homes of the stars and sites of murders, suicides, sexual shenanigans, and everyday deviancy in LaLaLand.
🚇 D1 ✉ Departs from Orchid Street at Hollywood Boulevard (east side of Mann's Chinese Theater) ☎ 323/469–4149 🕐 Daily at noon (by reservation only). Also special nighttime tours 🚌 1 ♿ None 💰 Very expensive

HOLLYWOOD ENTERTAINMENT MUSEUM
Memorabilia, interactive exhibits and back lot tours offer a peek behind the scenes at this user-friendly film and movie museum. Chart the development of film technology and movie make-up, listen to taped interviews with famous actors and directors, create your own sound effects, and venture aboard the original set for the bridge of *Star Trek*'s "Starship Enterprise."
🚇 D1 ✉ 7021 Hollywood Boulevard, Hollywood ☎ 323/465–7900 🕐 Tue–Sun 10–6 🚌 1, 217 ♿ Very good 💰 Moderate

HOLLYWOOD ROOSEVELT HOTEL
A romantic rendezvous for Clark Gable and his wife, Carole Lombard, where Errol Flynn supposedly invented his own gin cocktail behind the barber shop, and where David Niven slept in the servants' quarters before his star was born, the Roosevelt mounts a display of photos and Hollywood memorabilia from film's early days through the 1940s: of greatest interest to film buffs.
🚇 D1 ✉ 7000 Hollywood Boulevard, Hollywood ☎ 323/466–7000 🕐 Daily 🚌 1 ♿ Few 💰 Free

HOLLYWOOD STUDIO MUSEUM
Cecil B. De Mille shot Hollywood's first full-length movie in this old horse barn in 1913. Moved from its site on Vine to the Paramount lot across from the Hollywood Bowl, it now houses film memorabilia and antique moviemaking equipment.
🚇 D1 ✉ 2100 N Highland Avenue, Hollywood ☎ 323/874–2276 🕐 Thu–Sun 11–4 🚌 420, 426 ♿ Few 💰 Inexpensive

WARNER BROTHERS STUDIO VIP TOUR
The best behind-the-scenes tour for the serious movie buff. Small groups (reservations advised; no children under 10) tour backlot sets, watch actual productions in progress where possible, and learn about the nitty-gritty of moviemaking.
🚇 Off map, northwest ✉ 4000 Warner Boulevard, Burbank ☎ 818/954–1744 🕐 Mon–Fri 9–4; Sat 10 and 2 🚌 96 ♿ Few 💰 Very expensive

Lights! Camera! Action!
Dozens of TV shows in search of an audience give away free tickets through agencies such as LIGHTS! CAMERA! ACTION! (☎ 818/509–8497) and Audiences Unlimited (☎ 818/506–0043). You can also apply direct to CBS Studio Center (☎ 818/760–5000) for the likes of *Roseanne*; CBS Television City (☎ 323/852–2624) for *The Price is Right*; NBC Television (☎ 818/840–3537) for *The Tonight Show with Jay Leno*; Paramount Studios (☎ 323/956–5575) for *Frasier*; and Warner Bros Studios (☎ 818/954–1744) for *Murphy Brown* and *E.R.*

Charlie Chaplin statue in the Hollywood Roosevelt Hotel

LANDMARKS

Blots on the horizon

Two high-rise districts loom large on the horizon, though they fail to cut much of an architectural dash. At least Downtown can lay claim to the tallest building west of Chicago in the 73-story Library Tower, 633 W 5th Street. In West LA, Century City's gleaming towers (access from Avenue of the Stars) make a pretty show of reflecting the sunset in their blank glass faces, but the bland office-shopping-entertainment complex is less than inspiring.

ANGEL'S FLIGHT
From 1901 to 1969 the world's shortest railway (total length 315 feet) ferried passengers up and down Bunker Hill. Fully renovated and returned to service, the historic funicular shuttles between Hill Street and California Plaza like a small black and orange bug.

➕ M7 ✉ Hill Street at 4th Street ☎ 213/626–1901 🕐 Daily 6:30AM–10PM 💲 Inexpensive

CALIFORNIA PLAZA
Atop Bunker Hill, Downtown's towering concrete and glass financial district, the billion-dollar California Plaza complex (masterplan by Arthur Erikson Architects) houses offices, a hotel, and MOCA (➤ 37). Be mesmerized by the dancing fountains, animated geysers that bounce and bubble to a multicolored light show at night.

➕ M7 ✉ Grand Avenue 🚌 DASH B 💲 Free

CAPITOL RECORDS TOWER
Welton Becket's 1954 tower for the company that can list Frank Sinatra and the Beach Boys in its back catalogue is one of Hollywood's most famous landmarks. Though the architect denied it was intentional, it certainly looks like a stack of records topped by a needle.

➕ E1 ✉ 1750 Vine Street, Hollywood 🚌 1, 210, 310, 426

CHIAT/DAY INC ADVERTISING BUILDING
Frank Gehry's 1985 advertising agency office is definitely one for the picture album. The entrance is flanked by a pair of giant, three-story-high black binoculars designed by Claes Oldenburg.

➕ Off map, west ✉ 340 Main Street, Venice 🚌 33, 333, SM1

City Hall, Beverly Hills

CITY HALL
This Downtown monolith, the tallest building in the city from 1928 until 1959, still cuts an imposing figure. Once "destroyed" by Martians in *War of the Worlds*, it is familiar as the *Daily Planet* building in the *Superman* TV series, the police HQ from *Dragnet*, and has starred in dozens of other TV series and films.

➕ N7 ✉ 200 N Spring Street 🚌 Civic Center 🚌 DASH D

COCA-COLA BOTTLING FACTORY
This 1936 streamlined Moderne triumph by Robert Derrah resembles a giant ocean liner with

riveted port holes for windows, a "bridge" structure bearing the Coca-Cola logo and a nautical red, white, and blue trim.

➕ M10 ✉ 1334 S Central Avenue (at 14th Street) 🚌 53

MANN'S CHINESE THEATER

A Hollywood legend in its own right, the Chinese was built by Sid Grauman in 1927 to host extravagant premieres. The hodgepodge of pagoda roofs and twiddly towers, dragon motifs, Fu dogs, and temple bells is appealingly kitsch, and there is a splendid art deco interior.

➕ D1 ✉ 6925 Hollywood Boulevard, Hollywood ☎ 323/464–8111 🚌 1, 217

PACIFIC DESIGN CENTER

Beached just off La Cienega Boulevard, this enormous colored glass leviathan (1975) is affectionately known as the "Blue Whale" for obvious reasons. Actually, there are two buildings (one of them green) by Cesar Pelli and Gruen Associates offering 1.2 million square feet of showroom space.

➕ Off map, west ✉ 8687 Melrose Avenue (west of San Vicente), West Hollywood 🚌 10, 11

TAIL O' THE PUP

Just around the corner from the "Blue Whale" (above), you can grab a bite to eat *and* view a famous roadside landmark at this 1946 hotdog-shaped fast-food stand.

➕ Off map, west ✉ 329 San Vicente Boulevard (north of Beverly Boulevard, West Hollywood) 🚌 14

WATTS TOWERS

A bizarre beacon in this otherwise run-down neighborhood, these folk-art towers were built from scrap by Italian immigrant Simon Rodia between 1921 and 1954. Fashioned from steel rods, old bed frames, bottles, and more than 10,000 seashells, the central tower is almost 100 feet high. Guided tours recommended.

➕ Off map, south ✉ 1765 E 107th Street, Watts ☎ 323/847–4646 🚫 Closed for reconstruction

Hollywoodland

The famous Hollywood sign derives from a 1923 promotion when the word "Hollywoodland" was blazened across the Hollywood Hills to sell a residential development. The "land" was knocked off the sign in 1949, and the remaining 50-foot-high letters are probably the city's most recognizable landmark. There are good views from high points all over town, including the Griffith Observatory (➤ 32).

One of the towers at Watts built from scrap

55

HISTORIC BUILDINGS

See Top 25 Sights for
BRADBURY BUILDING (➤ 39)
EL PUEBLO DE LOS ANGELES, AVILA ADOBE
  (➤ 41)
GAMBLE HOUSE (➤ 44)
HOLLYHOCK HOUSE (➤ 34)

Mission survivors

Both LA's original Spanish missions still exist in the valleys that took their names. Southeast of Pasadena, the Mission San Gabriel Archangel, 537 W Mission Drive, San Gabriel (☎ 626/457–3048), was founded first in 1771. Although badly shaken by recent earthquakes, it is set in pretty gardens and the church has been reopened. The attractive Mission San Fernando Rey de España, at 15151 San Fernando Mission Boulevard, Mission Hills, appears in better condition, but has been largely reconstructed.

BILTMORE HOTEL

This grand old dame dates from 1923. Enter from Pershing Square to admire the beautifully restored Spanish Revival-style Rendezvous Court lobby.
➕ M7 ▢ 506 S Grand ▦ Pershing Square ▣ DASH B, C

ENNIS-BROWN HOUSE

The best of Frank Lloyd Wright's Maya-style concrete structures (1924) on a terrific site in the hills near Griffith Park. Privately owned, but occasionally open for tours by reservation.
➕ Off map, northwest ▢ 2655 Glendower Avenue, Los Feliz ☎ 323/660–0607 ▧ Expensive

LOS ANGELES CENTRAL LIBRARY

A Beaux-Arts treasure (1926, Goodhue and Winslow Sr.) ornamented with carved reliefs of great thinkers, writers, scientists, and choice *bons mots*. Historic 1930s murals in the Cook Rotunda.
➕ M7 ▢ 630 W 5th Street ☎ 213/228–7000 ◉ Mon, Thu–Sat 10–5:30; Tue–Wed noon–8; Sun 1–5. Tours Mon–Fri 12:30; Sat 11, 2; Sun 2 ▦ Pershing Square ▣ DASH A, B, C, F ♿ Good ▧ Free

ORPHEUM THEATRE

Fabulously restored 1911 vaudeville theater now operating as a cinema. The original Wurlitzer pipe organ is warmed up on Saturday mornings.
➕ M8 ▢ 842 S Broadway ☎ 213/239–0938 ◉ Call for current movie schedules ▣ 27, 28, 45, 46

Rudolph Schindler's house

SCHINDLER HOUSE

Rudolph Schindler's innovative 1921 design for California living. Its indoor/outdoor plan became the prototype for much Southern California vernacular architecture.
➕ Off map, west ▢ 835 N Kings Road, West Hollywood ☎ 323/651–1510 ◉ Wed–Sun 11–6 ♿ Few ▧ Inexpensive

UNION STATION

This Spanish Mission-style beauty was built by the railroad companies in 1939 (design by J. and D. Parkinson). View the lofty, barrel-shaped ceiling and Moorish tile trim of the main hall.
➕ N6/7 ▢ 800 N Alameda Street ▦ Union Station ▣ DASH B, D

GARDENS & GREEN SPACES

See Top 25 Sights for
GRIFFITH PARK (▶ 32)
**HUNTINGTON LIBRARY, ART COLLECTIONS
AND BOTANICAL GARDENS (▶ 46)**
**LOS ANGELES STATE AND COUNTY
ARBORETUM (▶ 47)**
RANCHO LOS ALAMITOS (▶ 43)

DESCANSO GARDENS
Glorious gardens covering 65 acres, including a
30-acre California live oak forest. Camellias
bloom spectacularly from January to March. (See
Pasadena Pops ▶ 82.)
🔟 Off map, northeast ✉ 1418 Descanso Drive, La Cañada (Verdugo
Boulevard exit off I-210/Foothill Freeway, northwest of Pasadena)
☎ 818/952–4400 🕐 Daily 9–4:30 except Christmas 🚌 177
🚹 Inexpensive

EXPOSITION PARK ROSE GARDEN
This fragrant spot boasts around 20,000 rose
bushes from some 200 varieties in a sunken
garden beside the Natural History Museum.
🔟 J11 ✉ Exposition Boulevard 🕐 Open site 🚌 DASH F/Expo
Park 🚹 Free

GREYSTONE PARK
The parklands surrounding oil millionaire
Edward Doheny's 1928 Gothic mansion
offer fine views over Beverly Hills.
🔟 Off map, west ✉ 905 Loma Vista Drive, Beverly Hills
☎ 310/550–4669 🕐 Daily 10–5; until 6 in summer
🚌 2, 3, 302 🚹 Free

VIRGINIA ROBINSON MANSION &
GARDENS
A hidden treasure of Beverly Hills, the
late society hostess Virginia Robinson's
Mediterranean-style villa is set in 6 acres
of lush gardens and groves with palms,
terraces and water features.
🔟 Off map, west ✉ 1008 Elden Way, Beverly Hills
☎ 310/276–5367 🕐 Tue–Fri by reservation only
🚹 Moderate

WILL ROGERS STATE HISTORIC PARK
There is plenty of space for kids to run
wild and picnic on this 186-acre hillside
ranch, the Western-style home of the
"Cowboy Philosopher." There are house
tours, a nature trail, and horses, stables,
and occasional polo games to watch.
🔟 Off map, west ✉ 14253 Sunset Boulevard, Pacific Palisades
☎ 310/454–8212 🕐 Park: daily 8–sunset. House: daily 10:30–4:30
🚌 2, 302 🚹 Moderate

Touring Eden
A landscape architect and a
landscape designer set up the
guide service Touring Eden
(☎ 818/769–2304) to squire
garden lovers around LA's
horticultural highlights. From
Malibu to Beverly Hills and up to
Pasadena, they offer expert and
enthusiastically guided tours for
individuals and groups.

*Virginia Robinson
Gardens*

ATTRACTIONS FOR CHILDREN

Miniature marvels

Wilshire Boulevard's "Miracle Mile" museums offer an interesting choice of attractions for kids, all within a couple of minutes' walk of each other. The fossils at the George C. Page Museum (➤ 50) appeal to young paleontologists; the shiny automobiles of the Petersen Automotive Museum (➤ 29) to child racers; and the Carol & Barry Kaye Museum of Miniatures, 5900 Wilshire Boulevard, Midtown (☎ 323/937–6464), exercises a mesmerizing dollshouse charm.

Shopfront detail, Hollywood Boulevard

HOLLYWOOD GUINNESS WORLD OF RECORDS MUSEUM
Trivia galore from The-Animal-with-the-Smallest-Brain-in-Proportion-to-Body-Size (a *Stegosaurus*) to the Most Biographed Female (Marilyn Monroe).
🔲 D1 🔲 6764 Hollywood Boulevard, Hollywood ☎ 323/463–6433 🕐 Daily 10–midnight 🚇 1 🎟 Moderate

KNOTT'S BERRY FARM
The nation's first theme park. Visit Camp Snoopy and the 1880s frontier Ghost Town; splash down in Wild Water Wilderness and ride the Jaguar roller coaster.
🔲 Off map, southeast 🔲 8039 Beach Boulevard, Buena Park ☎ 714/220–5200 🕐 Summer daily 9–midnight. Winter Mon–Fri 10–6; Sat 10–10; Sun 10–7 🚇 460 🎟 Very expensive

MUSEUM OF FLYING
The history of flight, vintage planes and interactive exhibits, including the first aircraft to circumnavigate the globe (in 1924).
🔲 Off map, southwest 🔲 2772 N Donald Douglas Loop, Santa Monica Airport ☎ 310/392–8822 🕐 Wed–Sun 10–5 🚇 SM8 🎟 Moderate

PACIFIC PARK
A seaside fairground with traditional rides (➤ 24), sideshows, and amusement arcades, plus virtual reality simulator adventures.
🔲 Off map, west 🔲 Santa Monica Pier, opposite Colorado Avenue ☎ 310/260–8744 🕐 Seasonal schedules 🚇 20, 22, 33, SM1, 7, 10 🎟 Charge per ride

SIX FLAGS CALIFORNIA
San Fernando Valley's theme park duo: Magic Mountain, renowned for its hair-raising thrill rides; and the Hurricane Harbor Water Park (summer season only).
🔲 Off map, northwest 🔲 Magic Mountain exit off I–5/Golden State Freeway ☎ 818/367–5965 🕐 Call for schedules 🚇 Metrolink to Santa Clarita, then SCT30 🎟 Very expensive

FREE ATTRACTIONS

Santa Monica beach and pier

CABRILLO AQUARIUM
Southern California marine life from the fantail sole known for its camouflage abilities to the bizarre grunion, a fish that comes ashore to breed.
➕ Off map, south ✉ Stephen White Drive (off Pacific Avenue), San Pedro ☎ 310/548–7562 🕐 Tue–Fri noon–5; Sat–Sun 10–5 🚌 446

FRANKLIN D. MURPHY SCULPTURE GARDEN
Sculptures by such artists as Arp, Hepworth, and Calder are sprinkled liberally over sunny lawns shaded by jacaranda trees. Works by Henry Moore, Miró, Maillol, and Rodin can be found on the tree-lined promenade.
➕ Off map, west ✉ UCLA Campus off Circle Drive East, Westwood 🕐 Open site 🚌 2, 302, SM1, 2, 3, 8, 12 (off Sunset Boulevard)

MULHOLLAND DRIVE
This winding mountain road with terrific views runs from Hollywood west past Malibu (with an unpaved section through Topanga State Park). Access to the eastern section off Laurel Canyon Boulevard; to the western section from Old Topanga Canyon Road.

Take a tour
The West Coast's biggest newspaper, the *Los Angeles Times*, offers free behind-the-scenes tours of its offices on weekdays (☎ 213/237–5757); and there are free tours of the attractively landscaped UCLA campus at Westwood (☎ 310/206–8147). On Pasadena's "Millionaires' Row," the Wrigley Gardens at Tournament House, 391 S Orange Grove Boulevard (☎ 626/449–4100), are open daily with free tours on Thursday afternoons from February to August.

59

BEACHES

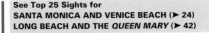
See Top 25 Sights for
SANTA MONICA AND VENICE BEACH (▶ 24)
LONG BEACH AND THE *QUEEN MARY* (▶ 42)

Hermosa Beach

HERMOSA BEACH
Slipped in between the other two major South Bay beaches, Manhattan and Redondo, Hermosa is renowned as LA's leading party beach. Lots of hanging out and volleyball for the well-toned.
🚫 Off map, southwest ✉ Off Pacific Coast Highway, Hermosa Beach 🚌 439

LEO CARRILLO STATE BEACH
On the LA County line beyond Malibu. Broad, mile-long sandy beach divided by Sequit Point. Surfing to the north; tide pools to entertain kids; and underwater caves revealed at low tide.
🚫 Off map, west ✉ Off Pacific Coast Highway (11 miles west of Malibu) 🚌 434

MALIBU SURFRIDER STATE BEACH
One of California's original surfing beaches, "The Bu" offers year-round waves but the best are during the late-summer southern swells (Aug–Sep).
🚫 Off map, west ✉ Off Pacific Coast Highway, Malibu 🚌 434

Off the beaten track
It is no easy task to escape the crowds. However, there are a few relatively quiet corners, namely a handful of small coves tucked into the steep, rocky bluffs of the Palos Verdes peninsula. On the north side, beyond Redondo Beach, try sandy Malaga Cove. Around to the south, near Lloyd Wright's Wayfarer's Chapel, Abalone Cove's rock pools provide entertainment and there is good snorkeling.

MANHATTAN BEACH
Fashionable beach suburb with cafés along the seafront. Good swimming, surfing, and games.
🚫 Off map, southwest ✉ Manhattan Beach Boulevard (off Pacific Coast Highway), Manhattan Beach 🚌 439

REDONDO BEACH
Hotel-lined beach with good swimming and a heated lagoon for children. Fishing from the pier.
🚫 Off map, southwest ✉ Off Pacific Coast Highway, Redondo Beach 🚌 439

WILL ROGERS STATE BEACH
Just north of Santa Monica, this is a good family beach with parking and fewer crowds.
🚫 Off map, west ✉ Off Pacific Coast Highway (opposite Sunset Boulevard), Pacific Palisades 🚌 434

ZUMA BEACH
LA's biggest beach and a hot favorite with the legendary San Fernando Valley Girls (and boys). Hip, action-packed, and crowded on weekends.
🚫 Off map, west ✉ Off Pacific Coast Highway (6 miles west of Malibu) 🚌 434

LOS ANGELES
where to...

AMERICAN RESTAURANTS

Prices

Average meal per person excluding drinks

$ = up to $15

$$ = $15 to $30

$$$ = $30 to $50

$$$$ = over $50

Except for luxury restaurants categorized as $$$$, where dinner could easily cost upwards of $70 for two people excluding wine (lunch will be less; typically around $40), dining in LA need not cost an arm and a leg. If you eat in reasonable restaurants, anticipate spending around $6–$8 per person for breakfast, $10 for lunch, and $15–$20 for dinner excluding drinks. Wherever you dine, a tip of at least 15 percent of the bill excluding wine is expected.

Opening times

All the listed restaurants are open daily for lunch and dinner unless otherwise stated. Angelenos generally lunch between 11:30 and 2, and have dinner between 6 and 9, though many restaurants open earlier and/or close later than these times.

CHASEN'S ($$$)

This legendary LA restaurant has seen the goings-on of film luminaries for over 60 years. Now in new digs, it retains much of its original décor, star-studded aura.

🚫 Off map, west ✉ 246 North Canon Drive, Beverly Hills ✉ 310/858–1200 🕐 Lunch Fri; dinner daily 🚌 20, 21, 22, 320

CITRUS ($$$)

Superstar-chef Michel Richard's casually chic American bistro offers creative, American versions of French classics, and some of the best desserts in LA.

🚫 D3 ✉ 6703 Melrose Avenue ✉ 213/857–0034 🕐 Lunch Mon–Fri; dinner Mon–Sat 🚌 10, 11

LAWRY'S THE PRIME RIB ($$$)

Aged prime rib, Yorkshire pudding, creamed spinach, and horseradish sauce. Clubby surroundings; established 1938.

🚫 Off map, west ✉ 100 N La Cienega Boulevard, Beverly Hills ✉ 310/652–827 🕐 Dinner only 🚌 20, 21, 22, 105

MORTON'S ($$$)

Stylish film-industry favorite packed with celebs grazing from the slightly healthful American menu.

🚫 Off map, west ✉ 8764 Melrose Avenue, West Hollywood ✉ 310/276–5205 🕐 Closed Sat lunch and Sun 🚌 10

NICOLA ($$–$$$)

Constructed with intriguing metal and wood design elements, this ethnically inspired American is a welcome Downtown oasis.

🚫 L7 ✉ 601 South Figueroa ✉ 213/485–0927 🕐 Lunch Mon–Fri; dinner Mon–Sat 🚌 20, 21, 22, 26

PACIFIC DINING CAR ($$–$$$)

This railway-theme restaurant offers superb steaks around the clock. Large portions, and the bill will reflect this—but most agree it's worth it.

🚫 L7 ✉ 1310 W 6th Street ✉ 213/483–6000 🚌 18, 20, 21, 200

THE RAYMOND ($$$)

Pretty, historic California bungalow with patios and a mixed menu.

🚫 Off map, northeast ✉ 1250 S Fair Oaks Avenue, Pasadena ✉ 818/441–3136 🕐 Closed Mon 🚌 483

SADDLE PEAK LODGE ($$$)

Rustic and romantic hunting lodge hideaway in the Santa Monica Mountains. Excellent game dishes in season.

🚫 Off map, northwest ✉ 419 Cold Canyon Road, Calabasas (San Fernando Valley) ✉ 310/456–7325 🕐 Dinner Wed–Sun and Sun brunch

VIDA ($$$)

Don't let names such as "verano escargot," or "sweet boy, poor bread" fool you: the internationally inspired American cuisine is excellent.

🚫 Off map, west ✉ 1930 Hillhurst Avenue ✉ 213/660–4445 🕐 Dinner daily 🚌 180, 181

CONTEMPORARY RESTAURANTS

CHAYA BRASSERIE ($$$)

Minimalist with a Japanese sensibility that's also evident in the innovative, intriguing East-meets-West menu.

⊞ Off map, west ✉ 8741 Alden Drive, West Hollywood ☎ 310/859–8833 ⊙ Dinner only at weekends 🚌 14, 16

CHINOIS ON MAIN STREET ($$$)

Another bustling and stylish showcase for chef Wolfgang Puck's sensational California-Chinese creations.

⊞ Off map, west ✉ 2709 Main Street, Santa Monica ☎ 310/392–9025 ⊙ Closed for lunch Sat–Tue 🚌 33, SM1

FENIX ($$$)

Stunning art deco décor plus views and inventive California/ French menu. Noted wine cellar.

⊞ Off map, west ✉ Argyle Hotel, 8358 Sunset Boulevard, West Hollywood ☎ 213/848–6677 ⊙ Closed Sun dinner (bar menu available) 🚌 2, 3

THE IVY ($$$)

Reservations are a must for this film-folk hang-out. Great food and terrace dining.

⊞ Off map, west ✉ 113 N Robertson Boulevard, West Hollywood ☎ 310/274–8303 🚌 14, 16

JIRAFFE ($$$)

California-bistro fare, using the nearby Farmer's Market. Spare, airy, and casually chic.

⊞ Off map, west ✉ 502 Santa Monica Boulevard, Santa Monica ☎ 310/917–6671 ⊙ Lunch Tue—Fri; dinner Tue–Sun 🚌 Santa Monica bus 4

MICHAEL'S ($$$)

A California culinary pioneer, with an impressive contemporary art collection and lovely terrace.

⊞ Off map, west ✉ 1147 3rd Street, Santa Monica ☎ 310/451–0843 ⊙ Closed Sun–Mon and Sat lunch 🚌 20, 33, SM2

PANGAEA ($$$)

Sophisticated Pacific Rim cuisine. Superb seafood.

⊞ Off map, west ✉ Hotel Nikko at Beverly Hills, 465 S La Cienega Boulevard ☎ 310/246–2100 🚌 20, 21, 22

PARKWAY GRILL ($$$)

Cutting-edge California fare with Southwestern accents.

⊞ Off map, northeast ✉ 510 S Arroyo Parkway, Pasadena ☎ 818/795–1001 ⊙ Closed Sat lunch 🚌 401, 402

SPAGO ($$$)

Chef Wolfgang Puck's celebrity-studded haunt. Fine California cuisine includes the famous (but pricey) designer pizza.

⊞ Off map, west ✉ 1174 Horn Avenue, West Hollywood ☎ 310/652–4025 ⊙ Dinner only 🚌 2, 3

SPAGO OF BEVERLY HILLS ($$$$)

The Beverly Hills outpost of Wolfgang Puck's legendary chain remains the premier place to rub elbows with the rich and famous. Food excellent, atmosphere pure LA.

⊞ Off map, west ✉ 176 N Canon Drive, Beverly Hills ☎ 310/385–0880 ⊙ Lunch Mon–Sat; dinner daily 🚌 20, 21, 22, 320

California drinking

California wines make a fine accompaniment to almost any meal. Most come from the 400 or so wineries located in the Napa and Sonoma valleys north of San Francisco, where common grape varieties include Cabernet Sauvignon and Chardonnay, as well as California's unique varietal, Zinfandel, used to produce red, white, and pink wines. Winemakers' names to watch for include Beringer, Charles Krug, Christian Brothers, Inglenook, Lytton Springs, Ridge, Stag's Leap, and also *méthode champenoise* sparkling wines from Domaine Chandon.

FRENCH & ITALIAN RESTAURANTS

Celebrity hosts

The latest craze among Hollywood folk is owning your own restaurant. While Sly, Bruce, and Arnie conquer the world with Planet Hollywood and Thunder Roadhouse, Steven Spielberg and Jerry Katzenberg are riding high with DIVE! (► 69), Dan Ackroyd has a finger in the pie at the House of Blues (► 69), and Arnie crops up again with wife, Maria Shriver, at Schatzi on Main in Santa Monica.

FRENCH

THE DINING ROOM ($$$)

Beautiful formal dining room serving elegant cuisine. Lengthy wine list; polished service.
🔲 Off map, west ✉ Regent Beverly Wilshire Hotel, 9500 Wilshire Boulevard, Beverly Hills ☎ 310/274–8179 🚍 20, 21, 22

L'ORANGERIE ($$$)

Grand French restaurant with palatial décor, impeccable service and a modern-classic menu. Terrace dining.
🔲 Off map, west ✉ 903 N La Cienega Boulevard, West Hollywood ☎ 310/652–9770 🕐 Closed Mon, dinner only 🚍 4, 105

PATINA ($$$)

Exceptional modern French cuisine in a relaxed setting. Chef Joachim Splichal is probably the brightest star in LA's culinary firmament.
🔲 E3 ✉ 5955 Melrose Avenue, Hollywood ☎ 213/467–1108 🕐 Closed Mon lunch 🚍 10

PINOT BISTRO ($$$)

Try the interesting, well executed French Bistro cooking at famed chef Joachim Splichal's quaint restaurant.
🔲 Off map, west ✉ 12969 Ventura Boulevard, Studio City ☎ 818/990–0500 🕐 Lunch Mon–Fri; dinner daily 🚍 218, 424, 522, 425

TWIN PALMS ($$)

Named for the huge trees that poke out of the dining room into the sky, this country French restaurant continues to impress diners. Live music on weekends.
🔲 Off map, northwest ✉ 101 West Green Street, Pasadena ☎ 626/577–2567 🕐 Lunch, dinner daily 🚍 Pasadena buses 180, 181 and local shuttle

ITALIAN

ANGELI CAFFE ($$)

Locals love the antipasto as well as the wood-oven pizza at this hip and friendly restaurant.
🔲 C3 ✉ 7274 Melrose Avenue ☎ 213/936–9086 🕐 Lunch Mon–Sat; dinner daily 🚍 10, 11

COCO PAZZO ($$$)

High-styled restaurant in LA's chicest hotel; a favorite for its inventive northern Italian fare.
🔲 Off map, northeast ✉ 8440 Sunset Boulevard, West Hollywood ☎ 213/848–6000 🕐 Breakfast Mon–Fri; lunch, dinner daily 🚍 2, 3

DRAGO ($$-$$$)

Celestino Drago delivers mouth-watering Italian fare to an affluent crowd at his casual flagship restaurant. Regulars favor Sicilian specialties.
🔲 Off map, west ✉ 2628 Wilshire Boulevard, Santa Monica ☎ 310/828–1585 🚍 20, 320

VALENTINO ($$$)

Piero Selvaggi provides heavenly cuisine and an extensive wine list with white-glove service. A top dining choice.
🔲 Off map, west ✉ 3115 Pico Boulevard, Santa Monica ☎ 310/829–4313 🕐 Lunch Fri; dinner Mon–Sat 🚍 Santa Monica bus 7, 14

ASIAN RESTAURANTS

CHAN DARA ($–$$)
Small, trendy Thai dining room. Spicy soups and curries, satay, and good noodles.
🖂 1511 N Cahuenga Boulevard, Hollywood ☎ 213/464–8585
🚌 2, 3

GINZA SUSHI ($$$$)
This temple of Japanese gastronomy probably offers the most exciting *sushi* experience outside of Japan—worth every cent of the outrageously high price tag. Surrender to the whims of chef Masa Takayama and you are in for an unforgettable meal.
➕ Off map, west 🖂 218 Via Rodeo, Beverly Hills
☎ 310/247–8939 🕐 Dinner Tue–Sat 🚌 20, 21, 22, 320

JOSS ($$)
Sleek Chinese restaurant serving several unusual specialties such as Mongolian lamb.
➕ Off map, west 🖂 9255 Sunset Boulevard, Hollywood
☎ 310/276–1886 🕐 Closed lunch on weekends 🚌 2, 3

KATSU ($$$)
Top *sushi* bar—the freshest and best. Minimalist décor.
➕ Off map, northwest 🖂 1972 N Hillhurst Avenue, Los Feliz ☎ 213/665–1891
🕐 Closed for lunch on weekends 🚌 26, 204

OCEAN SEAFOOD ($$)
Vast Cantonese restaurant serving affordable fresh seafood dishes, and *dim sum* among other favorites.
➕ N6 🖂 747 N Broadway ☎ 213/687–3088 🚌 DASH B

SEOUL JUNG ($$$)
Exquisite Korean cuisine, including traditional barbeque prepared at the table. Luxurious atmosphere, solicitous service.
➕ L7 🖂 Omni Hotel, 930 Wilshire Boulevard
☎ 213/688–7777 🕐 Lunch, dinner daily 🚌 18, 20, 21, 200

THOUSAND CRANES ($$$)
Fine Japanese cuisine, *sushi* and *tempura* counters, charming service, and views over a Japanese garden.
➕ N7 🖂 New Otani Hotel, 120 S Los Angeles Street, Little Tokyo ☎ 213/253–9255
🕐 Closed Sat lunch 🚌 DASH A

WOO LAE OAK OF SEOUL ($$)
The modern Korean cooking, finally out of Koreatown, attracts adventurous diners.
➕ Off map, west 🖂 170 N La Cienega Boulevard, Beverly Hills
☎ 310/652–4187 🚌 20, 21, 22, 105

YUJEAN KANG'S GOURMET CHINESE CUISINE ($$)
Chef Yujean Kang has built a reputation around his unusual and intriguing Chinese cuisine, with such dishes as "pictures in the snow." Excellent wine list.
➕ Off map, northeast 🖂 67 North Raymond Avenue, Pasadena ☎ 626/585 0855
🕐 Lunch, dinner daily 🚌 187

Snack stops
Dim sum (Chinese dumplings) and noodle dishes make an inexpensive lunchtime treat. A quick bite can turn into a veritable feast at such notable dim sum parlors as Chinatown's Mandarin Deli 🖂 727 N Broadway, or Grandview Gardens 🖂 944 N Hill Street. For an affordable sushi blowout, make tracks for the all-you-can-eat sushi counter at Lighthouse Buffet 🖂 201 Arizona Avenue, Santa Monica.

MEXICAN & SOUTHWESTERN RESTAURANTS

A-maizing

Ground corn (*maíz* in Spanish) is a Mexican staple, and the chief ingredient of *tortillas*, the ubiquitous cornmeal pancakes that turn up in any number of guises on Mexican menus. Some of the most common varieties are soft, folded *burritos*, stuffed and deep-fried *enchiladas*, crescent-shaped, deep-fried *quesadillas* filled with cheese and chillies (a useful vegetarian option), and crispy folded *tacos* (*taco* literally means "snack" in Mexico).

AUTHENTIC CAFE ($–$$)

At this highly popular café sprinkled with New Mexican paraphernalia long lines build. The draw is Southwestern fare that is delicious, inventive, and authentic. Friendly.
✚ Off map, south ✉ 7605 Beverly Boulevard, Melrose-La Brea ☎ 213/939–4626 ◷ Lunch, dinner daily ▣ 14, 212

BARNEY'S BEANERY ($–$$)

Friendly roadhouse-style diner serving generous portions of Tex-Mex fare and hamburgers plus a lengthy beer menu, a bar, and pool table.
✚ Off map, west ✉ 8447 Santa Monica Boulevard, West Hollywood ☎ 213/654–2287 ▣ 4

BORDER GRILL ($$)

Great Mexican food with an inventive twist and a loud, eclectic crowd. Always packed.
✚ Off map, west ✉ 1445 4th Street, Santa Monica ☎ 310/451–1655 ◷ Dinner only ▣ 4, SM1, 7, 10

EL CHOLO ($$)

LA institution (est 1927) serving Mexican fare in hacienda-style surroundings with patio tables.
✚ Off map, west ✉ 1121 S Western Avenue, Midtown ☎ 213/734–2773 ▣ 30, 31

EL TORITO GRILL ($$)

Busy, fun place offering a wide range of Mexican and Southwestern dishes washed down with tequila.
✚ Off map, west ✉ 9595 Wilshire Boulevard, Beverly Hills ☎ 310/550–1599 ◷ Daily. Closed Thanksgiving, Christmas ▣ 20, 21, 22

LA GOLONDRINA ($$)

Classic Mexican joint in El Pueblo. *Mariachi* musicians and *margaritas*.
✚ N6 ✉ W-17 Olvera Street ☎ 213/628–4349 🚇 Union Station ▣ DASH B

MERIDA ($)

Small and friendly local Mexican restaurant serving Yucatan specialties. Patio.
✚ Off map, northeast ✉ 20 E Colorado Boulevard, Pasadena ☎ 818/792–7371 ▣ 483

REBECCA'S ($$$)

Frank Gehry was the architect, and suspended metal crocodiles from the ceiling. The Mexican-inspired menu is equally fashionable .
✚ Off map, west ✉ 2025 Pacific Avenue, Venice Beach ☎ 310/306–6266 ◷ Dinner only ▣ 33

SONORA CAFÉ ($$$)

Sophisticated Southwestern cuisine and home-on-the-range décor.
✚ Off map, west ✉ 180 S La Brea Avenue, Midtown ☎ 213/857–1800 ◷ Closed Sat, Sun lunch ▣ 14

TEX-MEX PLAYA ($–$$)

Cheery *margarita*-fueled Tex-Mex cantina on the beach at Pacific Palisades.
✚ Off map, west ✉ 118 Entrada Drive, Santa Monica ☎ 310/459–8596 ▣ 434

MISCELLANEOUS SELECTION

BOOK SOUP BISTRO ($)

Literary types gather for book signings and readings, grilled vegetable soup, salads, and atmosphere.

➕ Off map, west ✉ 8800 Sunset Boulevard, West Hollywood ☎ 310/657–1072 🚌 2, 3

DC3 ($$)

California cuisine for plane-lovers. Fresh pasta, grilled seafood, and uninterrupted runway views.

➕ Off map, southwest ✉ 2800 Donald Douglas Loop North, Santa Monica Airport ☎ 310/399–2323 🕐 Closed Mon dinner, Fri dinner and Sat 🚌 SM8

DIAGHILEV ($$$$)

A formal, Russian-French classic with a Belle Epoque interior; draws favor for its exquisite caviar and updated Russian fare.

➕ Off map, west ✉ Wyndham Bell Age Hotel, 1020 N San Vincente Boulevard, West Hollywood ☎ 310/854–1111 🕐 Dinner Tue–Sat 🚌 2, 3

FIG TREE ($$)

Fresh grilled fish and vegetarian dishes served up on a quiet, sunny patio close to the beach.

➕ Off map, west ✉ 429 Ocean Front Walk, Venice Beach ☎ 310/392–4937 🚌 33

GORDON BIERSCH BREWERY ($$)

Alfresco dining and people-watching, beers made on the premises, and good California cuisine.

➕ Off map, northeast ✉ 41 Hugus Alley, Old Town Pasadena ☎ 818/449–0052 🚌 177

GREENBLATT'S ($)

A haven for homesick New Yorkers, Greenblatt's dishes up deli favorites from corned beef to cheesecake.

➕ B2 ✉ 8017 Sunset Boulevard, West Hollywood ☎ 213/656–0606 🚌 2

INN OF THE 7TH RAY ($$)

Laid-back New Age hangout in lovely setting. Vegetarian and wholefood menu plus special barbecued chicken.

➕ Off map, west ✉ 128 Old Topanga Road, Malibu ☎ 310/455–1311

MCCORMICK & SCHMICK'S ($$)

Downtown outpost of a popular chain of attractive, traditional-style fish restaurants.

➕ L7 ✉ First Interstate World Center, 633 W 5th Street (4th floor) ☎ 213/629–1929 🕐 Closed lunch on weekends 🚌 DASH B, C, D

ROCKENWAGNER ($$)

European ambience and beautifully prepared dishes using the freshest local ingredients.

➕ Off map, west ✉ 2435 Main Street, Santa Monica ☎ 310/399–6504 🕐 Closed Mon lunch 🚌 33, SM1

WATER GRILL ($$)

Renowned seafood restaurant with oyster bar and underwater-themed mural.

➕ M7 ✉ 544 S Grand Avenue, Downtown ☎ 213/891–0900 🕐 Daily. Closed Sat–Sun lunch 🚌 DASH B, E

Eating with children

LA's chic dining haunts are not particularly child friendly, but family restaurants and burger chains abound, particularly near Disneyland and around South Bay, and children love perching at the bar at one of the 1950s-style themed diners to slurp on a milkshake or munch fries. Always check if the restaurant has a children's menu.

Cafés & Coffee Shops

Sunday brunch

Each week when Sunday rolls around, Angelenos gear up to "do" brunch. Generally served from around 10 or 11 until 2, numerous restaurants throughout the city lay on a variation of the combination breakfast and lunch theme with a set-price menu. However, the most popular brunch spots tend to be found on the coast, and patio dining is at a premium.

CROCODILE CAFÉ ($)
One of a fast-growing chain of informal, California cuisine cafés specializing in gourmet pizzas, pasta, and salads.
⊕ Off map, west ✉ 101 Santa Monica Boulevard, Santa Monica ☎ 310/394–4783 🚌 21, 22, 33, SM1, 7, 10

DUKE'S ($)
No-frills, entertainment industry hangout. Nothing over $10.
⊕ Off map, west ✉ 8909 Sunset Boulevard, West Hollywood ☎ 310/652–3100 🚌 2, 3

ED DEBEVIC'S ($$)
1950s theme diner with wacky waitresses, burgers, chili, and calorific pies.
⊕ Off map, west ✉ 134 N La Cienega Boulevard, Beverly Hills ☎ 310/659–1952 🚌 20, 21, 22, 105

GOOD STUFF ($)
South Bay health food outpost with ocean views and a clientele of lycra-clad roller-bladers.
⊕ Off map, southwest ✉ 1286 The Strand, Hermosa Beach ☎ 310/374–2334 🚌 439

POW WOW ESPRESSO BAR ($)
A handy stop on Sunset serving gourmet coffees, sandwiches and pastries.
⊕ Off map, west ✉ 8868 Sunset Boulevard, West Hollywood ☎ 310/854–0668 🚌 2, 3

SIDEWALK CAFÉ ($)
Great people-watching from the beachfront terrace. Sandwiches, salads, tostadas, burgers.
⊕ Off map, west ✉ 1401 Ocean Front Walk, Venice Beach ☎ 310/399–5547 🚌 33

THE SOURCE ($)
Longstanding vegetarian and vegan landmark on "The Strip."
⊕ Off map, west ✉ 8301 Sunset Boulevard, West Hollywood ☎ 213/656–6388 🚌 2, 3

VILLAGE COFFEE SHOP ($)
Laid-back, friendly haunt of creative types in the Hollywood Hills; good home-cooked food.
⊕ Off map, northwest ✉ 2695 N Beachwood Drive, Hollywood ☎ 213/467–5398 🕙 Closed Sun 🚌 208

WOLFGANG PUCK CAFÉ ($)
Sample abbreviated versions of the master's California-Asian fusion fare. Also Santa Monica and Universal City.
⊕ B2 ✉ 8000 Sunset Boulevard, West Hollywood ☎ 213/650–7300 🚌 2, 3

WORLD CAFÉ ($–$$)
Busy restaurant/bar with a good line in wood-fired pizzas, pastas, and vegetarian dishes.
⊕ Off map, west ✉ 2820 Main Street, Santa Monica ☎ 310/392–1661 🚌 33, SM1

GRAB A BITE TO EAT

BELMONT BREWING COMPANY ($)
Home-brewed beer and casual American menu. Dine out on the beachfront terrace.
✚ Off map, south ✉ 25 39th Place, Long Beach ☎ 562/433–3891 🚌 LBT 121

CANTER'S ($)
Classic Fairfax District deli serving kosher specials, huge pastrami sandwiches, and waitress banter 24 hours a day.
✚ B4 ✉ 419 N Fairfax Avenue, Midtown ☎ 213/651–2030 🚌 14, 217

DIVE! ($)
Kids love this upscale sandwich shop—Steven Spielberg has a hand in the submarine theme.
✚ Off map, west ✉ Century City Shopping Center, 10250 Santa Monica Boulevard, West LA ☎ 310/788–3483 🚌 4, 22, 322

HOUSE OF BLUES ($$)
Popular and fun, this American theme restaurant specializes in Southern fare. Call ahead to find out about visiting chefs and gospel brunches.
✚ Off map, west ✉ 8439 Sunset Boulevard, West Hollywood ☎ 323/848–5100 🕐 Lunch Mon–Sat; dinner daily 🚌 2, 3, 429

KOKOMO ($)
Freshly baked muffins, deli sandwiches, steaming bowls of tasty gumbo, salads—all good reasons to brave the Farmers' Market.
✚ B4 ✉ Farmers' Market, 6333 W 3rd Street, Midtown ☎ 213/933–0773 🚌 16, 217

LA BREA BAKERY ($)
Although this bakery is attached to a terrific Italian restaurant (Campanile), the thing to go for is breakfast: Some of the best breads in the country come out of baker Nancy Silverton's ovens.
✚ Off map, west ✉ 624 S La Brea Avenue ☎ 213/938 1447 🕐 Breakfast, lunch, dinner daily 🚌 212

MANDARIN DELI ($)
Chinese *dim sum* (dumplings) and noodle dishes every which way.
✚ N6 ✉ 727 N Broadway ☎ 213/623–6054 🚌 DASH B

PASADENA BAKING COMPANY ($)
Great bakery in the Old Town. Muffins, croissants, pastries, sandwiches, and coffee on the terrace until late.
✚ Off map, northeast ✉ 29 E Colorado Boulevard, Pasadena ☎ 818/796–9966 🚌 401

PHILIPPE THE ORIGINAL ($)
Crusty fried bread, French dip sandwiches piled high with meats, cheese, and extra hot mustard. Heroic breakfasts, homemade pies.
✚ N6 ✉ 1001 N Alameda Street ☎ 213/628–3781 🚉 Union Station 🚌 DASH B

PINK'S FAMOUS CHILI DOGS ($)
This takeout stand is an LA institution. Foot-long jalepeño dogs, burgers, and tamales until 2AM.
✚ C3 ✉ 6919 Melrose Avenue, Midtown ☎ 213/931–4223 🚌 10

Malls and markets
LA's numerous shopping malls, such as the Beverly Center (➤ 71) and Downtown's Seventh Marketplace (➤ 71), are a good source of cheap eats offering a wide choice of fast-food outlets as well as delis and ethnic takeout counters with shared seating. The touristy-tacky Farmers' Market (➤ 71) has a wide choice of budget eateries, particularly popular on weekends, while the down-to-earth Grand Central Market (➤ 38) is the best place to find budget bites Downtown bar none.

SHOPPING DISTRICTS

The Garment District

Downtown's Garment District is a great spot for bargain hunters. Centered on Los Angeles Street (between 8th and 11th Streets). It offers dozens of discount retail, jobber, and manufacturers' outlet stores with fashion buys at bargain prices. Check out the Cooper Building, one of Southern California's largest outlet and discount fashion centers, at 860 Los Angeles Street, with more than 50 stores spread over six floors.

MAIN STREET

Hip boutiques, arty design and novelty shops helpfully interspersed with good restaurants.

➕ Off map, west ✉ Main Street (between Hollister and Rose avenues), Santa Monica 🚌 SM1, 8, 10

MELROSE AVENUE

A 3-mile strip of the esoteric and exotic from cutting-edge fashion and retro boutiques to galleries and gift stores. Riveting window-shopping, dining, and entertainment.

➕ D3 ✉ Melrose Avenue (between Highland Avenue and Doheny Drive), Hollywood 🚌 10, 11

MONTANA AVENUE

Ten blocks of super up-scale shopping for the woman with almost everything. Designer boutiques, elegant home-decorating emporiums, and luxurious beauty salons.

➕ Off map, west ✉ Montana Avenue (between 7th and 17th streets), Santa Monica 🚌 SM3, 9

OLD TOWN PASADENA

Bisected by Colorado Boulevard, this attractively restored 12-square block enclave offers an appealing selection of boutiques, galleries, gift stores, and eateries.

➕ Off map, northeast ✉ Colorado Boulevard (between Arroyo Parkway and Delacey Avenue), Pasadena 🚌 177, 180, 181, 401, 402, 483, 485

RODEO DRIVE

LA's answer to London's Bond Street and Rome's Via Condotti, Rodeo Drive is a gold-plated shopping experience. Top designer clothes and accessories, a surfeit of jewelers, and chic retail complexes.

➕ Off map, west ✉ Rodeo Drive, Beverly Hills 🚌 4, 20, 21, 22

SUNSET PLAZA

An exclusive little cluster of ultra-fashionable boutiques and sidewalk bistros on "The Strip."

➕ Off map, west ✉ Sunset Boulevard (between San Vicente and La Cienega boulevards), West Hollywood 🚌 2, 3

3RD STREET PROMENADE

Shoppers, street musicians, and street vendors jostle along the pedestrianized Promenade with many shopping, dining, and entertainment options.

➕ Off map, west ✉ 3rd Street (between Wilshire Boulevard and Broadway), Santa Monica 🚌 4, 20, 22, SM1, 2, 3, 7, 8, 9, 10

WESTWOOD VILLAGE

Outdoor cafés add to the appeal of this Mediterranean-style "Village" offering fashion, sports, and music stores designed to appeal to students from the neighboring UCLA campus (▶ 18).

➕ Off map, west ✉ Westwood Boulevard (off Wilshire Boulevard), Westwood 🚌 20, 21, 22, SM1, 2, 3, 8, 12

SHOPPING CENTERS & MALLS

BEVERLY CENTER
Major league mall with more than 160 upscale fashion, department, and specialty stores, and cinemas and restaurants.
✚ Off map, west ✉ 8500 Beverly Boulevard, West Hollywood ☎ 310/854–0070 🚌 14, 16, 105, 220

CENTURY CITY SHOPPING CENTER & MARKETPLACE
LA's premier outdoor shopping, dining, and entertainment complex, with some 140 stores.
✚ Off map, west ✉ 10250 Santa Monica Boulevard, West LA ☎ 310/277–3898 🚌 4, 22, 322

DEL AMO FASHION CENTER
Humongous South Bay retail center with 350 shops, 10 anchor stores, dining and cinemas.
✚ Off map, southwest ✉ Hawthorne Boulevard (at Carson), Torrance ☎ 310/542–8525

GLENDALE GALLERIA
Giant San Gabriel Valley mall featuring The Broadway, Nordstrom's, and J.C. Penney with some 250 other stores and restaurants.
✚ Off map, north ✉ 2148 Glendale Galleria, Glendale ☎ 818/240–9481 🚌 180, 181

LONG BEACH PLAZA
Part of the busy downtown Pine Avenue retail district: 140 stores with dining and entertainment.
✚ Off map, south ✉ 451 Long Beach Boulevard, Long Beach ☎ 310/435–8686

🚈 Metro Blue Line/Pine Avenue 🚌 60, 232

SANTA MONICA PLACE
Three stories of boutiques, accessories, kids' clothes, lingerie from Frederick's of Hollywood, Williams-Sonoma cookshop, plus a food court.
✚ Off map, west ✉ Broadway at 3rd Street, Santa Monica ☎ 310/394–5451 🚌 4, 20, 22, 33, SM1, 2, 3, 7, 8, 9, 10

SEVENTH MARKETPLACE
Relatively modest open-air Downtown mall with a brace of department stores and a food court.
✚ L7 ✉ 735 S Figueroa Street ☎ 213/955–7150 🚌 DASH A, E, F

SOUTH COAST PLAZA
Massive, state-of-the-art Orange County mall. US department stores, European designers, kids' entertainment.
✚ Off map, southeast ✉ 3333 Bristol Street, Costa Mesa ☎ 714/435–2000

UNIVERSAL CITYWALK
Eclectic gifts, souvenirs, and entertainment outside Universal Studios.
✚ Off map, northwest ✉ 1000 Universal Center Drive, Universal City ☎ 818/622–4455 🚌 420, 424, 425

WESTSIDE PAVILION
Chic selection of men's and women's fashions, gifts, dining and cinema.
✚ Off map, west ✉ 10800 W Pico Boulevard, West LA ☎ 310/474–6255 🚌 SM7, 8, 12, 13

Farmers' Market
Born in the 1930s Depression, at 6333 W 3rd Street, Midtown, when local farmers would bring their produce here in search of buyers, the market has metamorphosed into an LA institution. It's touristy, and tacky souvenirs abound, but you can still find fresh fruit and vegetables, butchers, bakers, deli counters, and great value fast food from coffee and donuts to po'boy sandwiches.

MEN'S & WOMEN'S CLOTHING

"Department Store Row"

As if Rodeo Drive were not enough to keep Beverly Hills' gold card-toting matrons occupied between lunches, LA's "Department Store Row" lies a mere stretch limo's length away. Neiman Marcus (✉ 9700 Wilshire Boulevard ☎ 310/550–5900), Saks Fifth Avenue (✉ 9600 Wilshire Boulevard ☎ 310/275–4211), and Barneys New York (✉ 9570 Wilshire Boulevard ☎ 310/276–4400) offer the full complement of fashions, furnishings, gifts, and cosmetics.

BIJAN USA

Casual and sporting menswear in a more accessible version of the wildly exclusive "by appointment only" store on the Penthouse level.

➕ Off map, west ✉ Rodeo Collection, 421 N Rodeo Drive, Beverly Hills
☎ 310/285–1800 🚌 4

THE COCKPIT

Packed floor to ceiling with Americana from leather flying jackets, jeans, and baseball caps to Harley Davidson bike boots, badges, and collectibles.

➕ Off map, west ✉ 9609 Santa Monica Boulevard, Beverly Hills ☎ 310/274–6900 🚌 4

DREAM DRESSER

Latex, leather, and downright lascivious gear created with dream weavers and exotic clubbers in mind.

➕ Off map, west ✉ 8444–50 Santa Monica Boulevard, West Hollywood ☎ 213/848–3480 🚌 4

FRED HAYMAN BEVERLY HILLS

A bastion of Beverly Hills high-fashion sportswear and Academy Award night frocks.

➕ Off map, west ✉ 273 N Rodeo Drive, Beverly Hills
☎ 310/271–3000 🚌 20, 21, 22

FRED SEGAL

Legendary and eternally hip Melrose specialty store complex. Sportswear and designer collections for men, women, and children, gifts, accessories, lingerie, and luggage.

➕ A3 ✉ 8100 Melrose

Avenue, West Hollywood
☎ 213/651–4129 🚌 10, 11

GIORGIO BEVERLY HILLS

Veteran Rodeo Drive designer and perfumier. Ladies-who-lunch, charming staff, and outrageous prices.

➕ Off map, west ✉ 327 N Rodeo Drive, Beverly Hills
☎ 310/274–0200 🚌 20, 21, 22

GUESS?

Fashionable and comfortable suits and casual clothing for men and women, plus great kidswear at several locations around town. Also outlet bargains in the Cooper Building (► 70, panel).

➕ Off map, west ✉ Unit 3, Century City Shopping Center, West LA ☎ 310/556–0123 🚌 4

JAY WOLF

Tucked away in a small courtyard, Wolf specializes in discreet and comfortable modern designer clothing (Paul Smith, Margaret Howell) for men and women.

➕ Off map, west ✉ 517 N Robertson Boulevard, West Hollywood ☎ 310/273–9893 🚌 10, 11, 220

TOMMY HILFIGER

Hilfiger has captured the LA celebrity crowd with a funky and glittery, Rock 'N' Roll collection created for pop and rock stars.

➕ Off map, west ✉ 468 N Rodeo Drive, Beverly Hills
☎ 310/888–0132 🚌 4

RETRO & SECONDHAND CLOTHING

AAARDVARKS' ODD ARK

Barnlike vintage clothing store. Dinner jackets from bandleader-flash to butler's tails, frocks and feather boas, accessories, and wig bin. Also in Pasadena and Venice.

✚ B3 ✉ 7579 Melrose Avenue, West Hollywood
☎ 213/655–6769 🚌 10, 11

AMERICAN RAG

Vast secondhand clothes and accessories emporium. Tuxes, grunge, ex-military great coats, '70s glam, and '80s unspeakable.

✚ Off map, west
✉ 150 S La Brea, Midtown
☎ 213/935–3154 🚌 14, 212, 316

AMERICAN VINTAGE

The "worn-out-West" look—previously loved denim, *Top Gun* aviator jackets, bowling shirts, aloha prints, plus US collectibles, vintage Zippos, and Native American jewelry.

✚ C3 ✉ 645 N Martel Avenue, West Hollywood
☎ 213/653–5645 🚌 10, 11

GOTTA HAVE IT

Behind an eye-catching playing card design façade, serried ranks of wildly assorted retro wear for guys and gals.

✚ Off map, west ✉ 1516 Pacific Avenue, Venice Beach
☎ 310/392–5949 🚌 SM7

IT'S A WRAP

Movie and television studio wardrobe departments offload their extravagances at this bulging Valley store. If an item's pedigree is star-studded, expect to pay.

✚ Off map, north ✉ 3315 W Magnolia Boulevard, Burbank
☎ 818/567–7366 🚌 183

PAPER BAG PRINCESS

One-of-a-kind vintage designer dresses and accessories from the likes of Alaïa, Yves St-Laurent, and Maud Frizon.

✚ Off map, west ✉ 8700 Santa Monica Boulevard, West Hollywood ☎ 310/358–1985
🚌 4

PARIS 1900

Antique lace, bows, and furbelows. Original Victorian and Edwardian collector's pieces for very special occasions. Open by appointment.

✚ Off map, west
✉ 2703 Main Street, Santa Monica ☎ 310/396–0405
🚌 33, SM1

STAR WARES ON MAIN

Thrift-shopping with a difference: all these cast-offs have a glittering pedigree. This is the place to pick up slinky frocks and other nearly new items culled from real stars' wardrobes.

✚ Off map, west
✉ 2817 Main Street, Santa Monica ☎ 310/399–0224
🚌 33, SM1

WASTELAND

Unmissable metal and mosaic façade fronting a funky collection of velvet, vinyl, and lurex delights, fluffy angora tops, and leopard-print hotpants.

✚ C3 ✉ 7428 Melrose Avenue, West Hollywood
☎ 213/653–3028 🚌 10, 11

Rocketing back in time

If you really get into the retro thing on Melrose Avenue, Johnny Rocket's, 7507 Melrose (corner of Gardner), West Hollywood, is the ultimate 1950s-style diner where you can order up a milkshake to match your new secondhand poodle skirt or strike a suitably Jimmy Dean pose over a hamburger and monopolize the juke box. And for something completely different, don't miss the wonderfully wacky flower petal-look street lamps diagonally across the street.

ANTIQUES & ART

Mission West

South Pasadena's turn-of-the-century Mission West shopping district is a favorite haunt for antique browsing. Along pretty, tree-shaded Mission Street there are more than half-a-dozen antiques dealers including furniture and collectibles at Mission Antiques ✉ 1018 Mission; paper memorabilia, such as postcards and magazines, at South Pasadena Mercantile Co. ✉ 1030 Mission; Yoko Japanese Antiques ✉ 1011 Mission; and linen and bric-a-brac at Hodgson's Antiques ✉ 1007 Mission.

ANTIQUARIUS

A great place for a browse: more than 30 shops specializing in antique jewelry, silver, art glass, and curios.
➕ Off map, west ✉ 8840 Beverly Boulevard, West Hollywood ☎ 310/274–2363 🚍 14

BERGAMOT STATION

This old trolley station now houses some 20 contemporary galleries dealing in an exciting range of art, sculpture, furniture, glass, and photography.
➕ Off map, west ✉ 2525 Michigan Avenue, Santa Monica ☎ 310/829–5854 🚍 SM9

BROADWAY GALLERY COMPLEX

Another Santa Monica arts enclave specializing in contemporary paintings, prints, and functional art such as furnishings with a distinctive California style.
➕ Off map, west ✉ 2018–2114 Broadway (between 20th & Cloverfield), Santa Monica 🚍 4, SM1, 10

ESTATE SALES & ANTIQUES

An elegant array of fine antique furniture and *objets d'art* including silver, glass, porcelain and jewelry.
➕ Off map, north ✉ 1012B Mission Street, Pasadena ☎ 626/799–8858 🚍 188, 256, 483

GEMINI G.E.L.

Prints by top American/US-based 20th-century artists including Rauschenberg, Jasper Johns, Hockney, and Richard Diebenkorn.
➕ Off map, west ✉ 8365 Melrose Avenue, West Hollywood ☎ 323/651–0513 🚍 10, 11

LOUIS STERN FINE ARTS

Well-respected gallery specializing in Impressionist, Latin American, 20th-century, and contemporary work.
➕ Off map, west ✉ 9002 Melrose Avenue, West Hollywood ☎ 310/276–0147 🚍 10, 11

MARGO LEAVIN GALLERY

An eye-catching knife sculpture skewers the Hilldale Street façade of this cutting-edge contemporary art gallery.
➕ Off map, west ✉ 812 N Robertson Boulevard, West Hollywood ☎ 310/273–0603 🚍 4, 220

SANTA MONICA ANTIQUE MARKET

150 stalls of antiques and collectibles from around the world. Silver, jewelry, books, crockery, clothing, and more.
➕ Off map, west ✉ 1607 Lincoln Boulevard, Santa Monica ☎ 310/314–4899 🚍 SM3

SANTA MONICA TRADING COMPANY

Teetering piles of vintage magazines, second-hand books, film posters, and appealing antique prints of fruit, fish, and flowers are crammed into this intriguing small shop.
➕ Off map, west ✉ 2705 Main Street, Santa Monica ☎ 310/392–4806 🚍 33, SM1

BOOKS & MUSIC

A DIFFERENT LIGHT
A huge selection of gay and lesbian literature. Evening readings; a good place for free listings magazines.
🚦 Off map, west 🖂 8853 Santa Monica Boulevard, West Hollywood ☎ 310/854–6601 🚌 4, 304

ACRES OF BOOKS
Rambling treasure trove of secondhand tomes on every conceivable topic.
🚦 Off map, south 🖂 240 Long Beach Boulevard, Long Beach ☎ 562/437–6980 🚇 Metro Blue Line/Long Beach Boulevard

BARNES & NOBLE
Standout among LaLaLand B&Ns; encyclopedic selection and bestseller discounts.
🚦 Off map, west 🖂 1201 3rd Street, Santa Monica ☎ 310/260–9110 🚌 4, 20, 22, SM1, 2, 3, 7, 8, 9, 10

BODHI TREE
The New Age bookstore where Shirley MacLaine got metaphysical.
🚦 Off map, west 🖂 8585 Melrose Avenue, West Hollywood ☎ 310/659–1733 🚌 10, 11

BOOK SOUP
This voluminous bookstore and news-stand has spawned a fashionable bistro next door. Classics to crime, reference books, and more; art history and movie sections are good.
🚦 Off map, west 🖂 8818 Sunset Boulevard, West Hollywood ☎ 310/659–3110 🚌 2, 3, 302, 429

BORDERS BOOKS AND MUSIC
An impressive selection of classic and contemporary literature and sounds, plus a handy in-store café.
🚦 Off map, west 🖂 1415 3rd Street Promenade, Santa Monica ☎ 310/393–9290 🚌 4, 20, 21, 22, SM1, 2, 3, 7, 8, 9, 10

HEAR MUSIC
Small but inviting and user-friendly music store with well-chosen rock, jazz, classical, folk, and world music.
🚦 Off map, west 🖂 1429 3rd Street Promenade, Santa Monica ☎ 310/319–9527 🚌 4, 20, 22, SM1, 2, 3, 7, 8, 9, 10

THE MYSTERIOUS BOOKSHOP
A gripping source of thrilling tomes.
🚦 Off map, west 🖂 8763 Beverly Boulevard, West Hollywood ☎ 310/659–2959 🚌 14

SMALL WORLD BOOKS & THE MYSTERY ANNEXE
Convenient beachfront emporium: everything from classics and a few foreign language books to beach vacation mysteries, sex 'n' sun 'n' shopping sagas.
🚦 Off map, west 🖂 1407 Ocean Front Walk, Venice Beach ☎ 310/399–2360 🚌 33

VIRGIN MEGASTORE
Like rival Tower Records (8801 Sunset) Richard Branson's Megastore encompasses the musical spectrum from obscure indie labels to Elgar.
🚦 A2 🖂 8000 Sunset Boulevard, West Hollywood ☎ 323/650–8666 🚌 2, 3, 302, 429

Whale of a design district
The interior design capital of the Pacific Rim, West Hollywood boasts a wealth of art and antiques galleries, plus around 300 specialty design stores and showrooms centered on the west end of Melrose Avenue and San Vicente boulevards. One unmissable sight here is Pacific Design Center (aka "The Blue Whale" for its size and color ► 55), which harbors more than 200 decorator showrooms offering furniture, fabrics, floor and wall coverings, lighting, and kitchen products. The showrooms are now open to the general public (Mon–Fri 9–5), though some may require an appointment and others are open "to the trade only"; still others have a designer on call to make the necessary referral.

Movie Memorabilia & Souvenirs

Oceanfront Walk

Looking for LA T-shirts, Dodgers Baseball caps, postcards, and other souvenir tat? Then make a beeline for Venice Beach's open-air bazaar where the stalls are piled high with cheap LA-themed goods, $5 sunglasses, microscopic bikinis, West Coast thrash CDs, and New Age tie-dye creations.

CHIC-A-BOOM

Huge selection of film and advertising posters, plus vintage magazines, TV and rock memorabilia including autographs, books, fanzines, photographs and posters..

➕ D3 ✉ 6817 Melrose Avenue, West Hollywood ☎ 323/931–7441 🚇 10, 11

CINEMA COLLECTORS

Mountains of memorabilia for the terminally star-struck.

➕ E2 ✉ 1507 Wilcox Avenue, Hollywood ☎ 323/461–6516 🚇 1, 217

COLLECTORS' BOOKSTORE

The "most comprehensive array of cinematic collectibles on the planet"—apparently—movie stills, posters, magazines, scripts..

➕ E1 ✉ 1708 N Vine Street, Hollywood ☎ 323/467–3296 🚇 1, 217

THE DISNEY STORE

Goofy, Donald, Mickey, and Minnie are joined by the Little Mermaid, the Lion King, and other newcomers in the great merchandise heist.

➕ Off map, west ✉ Unit 39, Century City Shopping Center, 10250 Santa Monica Boulevard, West LA ☎ 310/556–8036 🚇 4, 304

FANTASIES COME TRUE

Nearly-new and antique Disney collectibles from famous character toys and china figurines to buttons and posters.

➕ B3 ✉ 8012 Melrose Avenue, West Hollywood ☎ 323/655–2636 🚇 10, 11

LARRY EDMUNDS' BOOK SHOP

A small but rich trawling ground for cinematic bibliophiles stocking all sorts of film and theater-related tomes, plus posters and stills.

➕ D1 ✉ 6644 Hollywood Boulevard, Hollywood ☎ 323/463–3273 🚇 1, 217

MGM STUDIO STORE

Your chance to dress up as an MGM/UA production crew member in official logo-strewn jackets, caps, and script bags.

➕ Off map, west ✉ 2501 Colorado Avenue, Santa Monica ☎ 310/449–3300 🚇 SM9

SAMUEL FRENCH THEATER & FILM BOOKSHOP

For true aficionados and wannabe movie writers, this is the place to pick up specialist books and essential and obscure film and theater scripts. Knowledgeable staff.

➕ B2 ✉ 7625 Sunset Boulevard, West Hollywood ☎ 323/876–0570 🚇 2, 3

WARNER BROTHERS STUDIO STORE

Bugs Bunny and the Loony Tunes crew feature on all manner of souvenir paraphernalia.

➕ Off map, west ✉ 270 Santa Monica Place (4th & Broadway), Santa Monica ☎ 310/393–6070 🚇 4, 33

SPECIALTY STORES & GIFTS

DEL MANO GALLERY

A terrific array of innovative and affordable contemporary crafts ranging from jewelry and silverware to art glass, ceramics, and furnishings.

➕ Off map, northeast ✉ 33 E Colorado Boulevard, Pasadena
☎ 626/793–6648
🚌 180, 181

EVERY PICTURE TELLS A STORY

Captivating bookstore-gallery displaying original art and lithographs from children's books: Eric Carle, Tim Burton, Maurice Sendak.

➕ B4 ✉ 7525 Beverly Boulevard, Midtown
☎ 323/932–6070 🚌 14

HAMMACHER SCHLEMMER

Splendidly eccentric upscale gifts, from personal robots to the Best Nose Hair Trimmer, all tested and approved by the Hammacher Schlemmer Institute (est. 1848).

➕ Off map, west ✉ 309 N Rodeo Drive, Beverly Hills
☎ 310/859–7255 🚌 20, 21, 22

LA EYEWORKS

From the town that never removes its shades, face furniture for every occasion.

➕ C3 ✉ 7407 Melrose Avenue, West Hollywood
☎ 323/653–8255 🚌 10, 11

MODERN LIVING

Cool glassblock setting for dramatic modern furnishings from groovy Italians and the likes of Philippe Starck.

➕ A3 ✉ 8125 Melrose Avenue, West Hollywood
☎ 323/655–3899 🚌 10, 11

MOE'S FLOWERS

Need to say it with flowers? This corner shop brims over with orchids, lilies, roses, exotic and seasonal cut flowers, and foliage. Arrangements and deliveries to order.

➕ A3 ✉ 8101 Melrose Avenue, West Hollywood
☎ 323/653–5444 🚌 10, 11

SOOLIP PAPERIE & PRESS

Amazing stationery store: racks of colorful handmade papers, colored inks, hip pens, and desk accessories.

➕ Off map, west ✉ 8646 Melrose Avenue, West Hollywood
☎ 310/360–0545 🚌 10, 11

WANNA BUY A WATCH?

Vintage and contemporary timepieces from Bulova to Betty Boop, Tiffany dress watches, US military issue, plus antique diamond and art deco jewelry.

➕ C3 ✉ 7366 Melrose Avenue, West Hollywood
☎ 323/653–0467 🚌 10, 11

THE WOUND & WOUND TOY CO

A nostalgic array of windup cars, trains and trucks, plus robots, singing birthday cakes, and Etch-A-Sketch keyrings.

➕ C3 ✉ 7374 Melrose Avenue, West Hollywood
☎ 323/653–6703 🚌 10, 11

St. Elmo's Village

A hippy-funky alternative to the fashion victim chic on Melrose, this unlikely arts project in quiet suburbia—a group of old wooden bungalows with gardens full of cacti and sculpture—welcomes visitors on weekends. In the mural-covered courtyard, artists offer free workshops in sculpture, painting, and performance arts from 11AM on Saturdays.

🏠 4830 St. Elmo Drive (off South La Brea), Midtown
☎ 323/936–3595)

CLASSICAL MUSIC & PERFORMING ARTS

Tickets
Concert and theater tickets can be purchased direct through the venue, or through Ticketmaster (☎ 213/381–2000), which also supplies tickets to sporting events, and Ticket Time (☎ 310/473–1000).

Sightseeing concerts
Join the Da Camera Society (☎ 310/440–1351; membership not required) for an evening of chamber music in one of several intimate and historic sites around the city. The "Chamber Music in Historic Sites" series has visited the Biltmore Hotel, the Huntington Library, and the *Queen Mary* among others.

BECKMAN AUDITORIUM
Host to the excellent Cal Tech After Dark performing arts season, which features big names in theater, music, and dance.
➕ Off map, northeast ✉ 332 S Michigan Avenue, Pasadena ☎ 888–2–CALTECH 🚌 401

GEFFEN PLAYHOUSE
Neighborhood theater with a fine reputation, intimate enough to host one-man shows.
➕ Off map, west ✉ 10886 Le Conte Avenue, Westwood ☎ 310/208–5454 🚌 20, 21, 22, SM1, 2, 3, 8, 12

HOLLYWOOD BOWL
Much-loved outdoor venue for the Los Angeles Philharmonic's Symphony Under the Stars series (Jul–Sep) and other alfresco performances.
➕ Off map, northwest ✉ 2301 N Highland Avenue, Hollywood ☎ 323/850–2000 🚌 420

JAPAN AMERICA THEATER
Contemporary and traditional Japanese Noh plays and kabuki theater.
➕ N7 ✉ 244 S San Pedro Street, Little Tokyo ☎ 213/680–3700 🚌 DASH A

MUSIC CENTER
LA's chief performing arts complex includes the Dorothy Chandler Pavilion (home to the LA Philharmonic's winter season), the Ahmanson Theatre (musicals, drama, and comedy), and the Mark Taper Forum (experimental productions). It is also used by the Music Center Opera and the acclaimed Joffrey Ballet.
➕ M6 ✉ 135 N Grand Avenue ☎ 213/972–7211 🚇 Civic Center 🚌 DASH A, B

ODYSSEY THEATRE
One of the city's most highly regarded avant-garde theater companies offers ensembles, and visiting productions.
➕ Off map, west ✉ 2055 S Sepulveda Boulevard, West LA ☎ 310/477–2055 🚌 SM9

PASADENA CIVIC AUDITORIUM
Home of the Pasadena Symphony Orchestra, and a magnificent 1920s Moeller theater organ. Also various theater and dance events.
➕ Off map, northeast ✉ 300 E Green Street, Pasadena ☎ 626/449–7360 🚌 401

SHUBERT THEATER
Century City's saving grace if you happen to be a fan of lavish big-production musicals.
➕ Off map, west ✉ 2020 Avenue of the Stars, Century City, West LA ☎ 800–447–7400 🚌 4

UCLA CENTER FOR THE PERFORMING ARTS (WADSWORTH THEATER)
Off-campus facility offering more than 200 music and dance events a year from home-grown and visiting performers.
➕ Off map, west ✉ 10920 Wilshire Boulevard, Westwood ☎ 310/825–2101 🚌 20, 21, 22, SM2

ROCK, JAZZ & BLUES

THE BAKED POTATO
One of LA's best contemporary jazz spots. The stuffed baked potatoes aren't bad either.
➕ Off map, northwest
✉ 3787 Cahuenga Boulevard (at Lankershim), Studio City
☎ 818/980–1615 🚌 420

B B KING'S BLUES CLUB
Restaurant and club serving Delta-style food and live blues, occasionally from the master himself. Gospel brunch on Sundays.
➕ Off map, northwest
✉ Universal City Walk, Universal City ☎ 818/622–5464 🚌 420, 424, 425, 522

HOUSE OF BLUES
This tin-shack theme restaurant on Sunset attracts massive lines and a generous sprinkling of celebs for southern food and headline blues-rock acts.
➕ Off map, west ✉ 8430 Sunset Boulevard, West Hollywood ☎ 323/848–5100
🚌 2, 3

M BAR & GRILL
California bar and grill that supplements good food with nightly jazz, blues, and alternative music sessions.
➕ Off map, south ✉ 213A Pine Avenue, Long Beach
☎ 562/435–2525 🚆 Blue Line/Pine Avenue 🚌 60

MCCABE'S GUITAR SHOP
Guitar store by day, R&B-rock-jazz-folk showcase on Friday and Saturday nights with some pretty impressive

names. Intimate, informal, alcohol-free.
➕ Off map, west ✉ 3101 W Pico Boulevard, Santa Monica
☎ 310/828–4403 🚌 SM7

THE MINT
Longstanding small blues bar with a faithful following and great music and atmosphere.
➕ Off map, west ✉ 6010 W Pico Boulevard, Midtown
☎ 213/954–9630 🚌 30

THE ROXY
Small, steamy rock venue popular with the in-crowd, showcasing major recording acts and new bands via a sound system that knocks your socks off.
➕ Off map, west ✉ 9009 Sunset Boulevard, West Hollywood ☎ 310/276–2222
🚌 2, 3

THE VIPER ROOM
Co-owned by Johnny Depp, the Viper draws cool crowds and big names. Jam and dance nights.
➕ Off map, west ✉ 8852 Sunset Boulevard, West Hollywood ☎ 310/358–1881
🚌 2, 3

WHISKY A GOGO
Though there is less "Go-Go" these days, this Sunset Strip stalwart is still a haven for hard rockers.
➕ Off map, west ✉ 8901 Sunset Boulevard, West Hollywood ☎ 310/652–4202
🚌 2, 3

Opening times
Most music bars are open nightly from around 9PM until 2AM. Headline acts tend to go on after 11PM, when the clubs start to liven up. Clubs and music bars are often closed on Sunday and Monday nights. Call ahead.

NIGHTCLUBS

Club circuit

For the dedicated clubber with plenty of stamina and deep pockets, LA NightHawks (☎ 310/392–1500) can arrange a VIP night on the town. Limousine transportation and no-hassle entry to a host of music, cabaret, dance, and comedy clubs.

ARENA
Huge dance club in a former warehouse once used for storing ice. Features theme nights from house and hip-hop to Latino. Live bands and DJs (Thu–Sun)
🔲 D3 ✉ 6655 Santa Monica Boulevard, Hollywood
☎ 323/462–0714 🚌 4, 420

CINEGRILL
Sleek art deco interior and an eclectic cabaret running the gamut from jazz to comedy. Deservedly popular.
🔲 D1 ✉ Hollywood Roosevelt Hotel, 7000 Hollywood Boulevard, Hollywood
☎ 213/466–7000 🚌 1

CRUSH BAR
Casual club with a retro heart that beats to the Motown and soul sound of 60s and '70s. Great dancing; reggae and hip-hop nights.
🔲 E2 ✉ 1743 N Cahuenga Boulevard, Hollywood
☎ 323/461–9017 🚌 1

FLORENTINE GARDENS
A dressy young clientele frequents this hip danceteria (Fri–Sun) with cool DJs and free buffet.
🔲 F1 ✉ 5951 Hollywood Boulevard, Hollywood
☎ 323/464–0706 🚌 1, 217

THE GATE
Chic dinner-dance club with music ranging from techno to hip-hop. Outdoor patios and California cuisine.
🔲 Off map, west ✉ 643 N La Cienega Boulevard, West Hollywood ☎ 310/289–8808
🚌 10, 11

MAYAN
A fashionably dressy crowd swings to salsa and disco in an exotic former theater Downtown.
🔲 L8 ✉ 1038 S Hill Street ☎ 213/746–4287 🚌 DASH D

THE PALACE
Staggeringly loud sound system, two dance floors, four bars, opposite Capitol Records Building. Hip-hop, house, R&B and retro (Thu–Sat).
🔲 E1 ✉ 1735 N Vine Street, Hollywood ☎ 323/462–3000
🚌 1, 217

THE PROBE
New wave, industrial, Brit pop and 1980s disco madness nights, plus a well-attended gay men's party on Saturdays.
🔲 D3 ✉ 836 N Highland Avenue, Hollywood
☎ 323/461–8301 🚌 10, 11

RAGE
Packed West Hollywood gay club for boys serving Top 40, house, Latin and progressive, drag comedy and variety.
🔲 Off map, west ✉ 8911 Santa Monica Boulevard, West Hollywood ☎ 310/652–7055
🚌 4, 304

THE ROXBURY
A night out with "the real Beverly Hills 90210 set." Dress up and party; live music, disco, and five bars.
🔲 Off map, west ✉ 8225 Sunset Boulevard, West Hollywood ☎ 213/656–1750
🚌 2, 3

BARS

BARNEY'S BEANERY
Convivial bar with a pool table and lengthy beer menu squeezed up against a Tex-Mex dining room (▶ 66).
➕ Off map, west ✉ 8447 Santa Monica Boulevard, West Hollywood ☎ 323/654–2287 🚌 4, 304

CASEY'S BAR & GRILL
Popular in the early evening with Downtown office workers. Happy hour and piano music.
➕ M7 ✉ 613 S Grand Avenue ☎ 213/629–2353 🚌 DASH B, C, E

CAT 'N' FIDDLE PUB
Lively young crowd comes to enjoy the outdoor patio and English beer on tap.
➕ E2 ✉ 6530 Sunset Boulevard, Hollywood ☎ 323/468–3800 🚌 2, 3

CHEZ JAY
Laid-back neighborhood beach bar with a broad clientele and a great juke box.
➕ Off map, west ✉ 1657 Ocean Avenue, Santa Monica ☎ 310/395–1741 🚌 20, 22, 33, SM1, 10

GOTHAM HALL
Stylish pool hall in the pedestrian heart of Santa Monica. Good people-watching in the bar; restaurant.
➕ Off map, west ✉ 1431 3rd Street Promenade, Santa Monica ☎ 310/394–8865 🚌 20, 22, 33, SM2, 3, 8, 9

HARVELLE'S
Westside neighborhood bar-cum-terrific blues club.
➕ Off map, west ✉ 1432 4th Street, Santa Monica ☎ 310/395–1676 🚌 4, SM1, 9, 10

MOLLY MALONE'S IRISH PUB
Venerable Irish-American institution. Guinness, darts, and Irish music.
➕ Off map, west ✉ 575 S Fairfax Avenue (south of Melrose Avenue), Midtown ☎ 323/935–1577 🚌 10, 11, 217

MUSSO & FRANK
Hollywood's oldest and most celebrated bar and grill.
➕ D2 ✉ 6667 Hollywood Boulevard, Hollywood ☎ 323/467–7788 🚌 1, 217

REGENT BEVERLY WILSHIRE
Dark, clubby bar with capacious leather seating and cigar-chomping clientele.
➕ Off map, west ✉ 9500 Wilshire Boulevard, Beverly Hills ☎ 310/275–5200 🚌 21, 22

SKY BAR
Glamorous Mondrian Hotel (▶ 84) poolside bar with fantastic city views. Open only to hotel guests and visitors with reservations.
➕ Off map, west ✉ 8440 Sunset Boulevard, West Hollywood ☎ 323/650–8999 🚌 2, 3, 302, 429

YE OLDE KING'S HEAD
Popular with local Brits. Draft beer, darts, pub grub, and heroic English breakfasts.
➕ Off map, west ✉ 116 Santa Monica Boulevard, Santa Monica ☎ 310/451–1402 🚌 4, 20, 22, 33, SM1 7, 10

Liquor laws
Bars can legally open at any time between 6AM and 2AM, though most open their doors around 11AM and close around midnight (later on Fridays and Saturdays). Licensed restaurants can serve alcohol throughout their hours of business except between 2AM and 6AM. To buy or consume alcohol legally in California, you must be 21 or older. Youthful-looking patrons may well be asked to show proof of age.

OTHER AFTER-DARK IDEAS

Catch a movie

New-release Hollywood movies often hit the screens in LA before they turn up in other parts of the country. To catch the latest releases check what's on at the multi-screen Universal City 18 Cinemas (☎ 818/508–0588), or take a stroll around Westwood Village, where half-a-dozen theaters offer everything from first-run movies to the classics. One of the best repertory cinemas screening art-house and foreign-language offerings is the Nuart Theater (✉ 11272 Santa Monica Boulevard, at Sawtrelle Avenue, West LA ☎ 310/478–6379).

BOB'S BIG BOY

Serried ranks of LA's coolest customized hot rods wheel up at this Valley diner on a Friday night. It's the Petersen (▶ 29) for real.
⊞ Off map, northwest
✉ 4211 Riverside Drive, Burbank ☎ 818/843–9334

COMEDY & MAGIC CLUB

Lively spot with stand-up comedy (occasional big names) spliced with magic acts.
⊞ Off map, southwest
✉ 1018 Hermosa Avenue, Hermosa Beach
☎ 310/372–1193 🚍 439

COMEDY STORE

Three stages showcase funsters who are up-and-coming, have made it or are just plain HUGE. One of the city's premier clubs.
⊞ Off map, west 🚍 8433 Sunset Boulevard, West Hollywood ☎ 323/656–6225 🚍 2, 3

COUNTRY STAR

A themed restaurant for country music fans serving downhome fare and country star memorabilia and music; interactive video booths are a plus.
⊞ Off map, northwest ✉ By Universal Studios entrance, Universal City
☎ 818/762–3939 🚍 420

GRIFFITH PARK OBSERVATORY

Spectacular views of the city and no charge for stargazing through the Observatory's 12-inch telescope (▶ 32).
⊞ Off map, northwest
✉ 2800 Observatory Road, Griffith Park
☎ 323/664–1181 🚍 69

GROUNDLINGS THEATER

Talented improvisational comedy troupe in short-run shows plus new talent nights.
⊞ C3 ✉ 7307 Melrose Avenue, West Hollywood
☎ 213/934–9700 🚍 10, 11

THE IMPROV

A popular new-material testing ground for big-name comics.
⊞ A2 ✉ 8162 Melrose Avenue, West Hollywood
☎ 213/651–2583 🚍 10, 11

MOONLIGHT TANGO CAFE

Nostalgic 1930s/40s-style Hollywood supper club locked in the Swing era with dining and dancing in the old-fashioned way.
⊞ Off map, northwest
✉ 13730 Ventura Boulevard, Sherman Oaks
☎ 818/788–2000 🚍 424, 425, 522

PASADENA POPS

Summer concerts in Descanso Gardens (▶ 57). Bring a picnic or order one with your ticket.
⊞ Off map, northeast
✉ 1418 Descanso Drive, La Canada ☎ 818/952–4401

WIZARDZ

A nightclub featuring magicians, tarot card readers, fortunetellers, and dinner shows with laser displays.
⊞ Off map, northwest
✉ CityWalk, Universal City
☎ 818/506–0066 🚍 420

GYMS, SPAS & SPORTS

AIDA THIBIANT EUROPEAN DAY SPA

A rollcall of Hollywood's most glamorous female movie stars come here for massage, facials, manicures, makeup, and skin treatments.

➕ Off map, west ✉ 449 N Cañon Drive, Beverly Hills ☎ 310/278–7565 🚌 3, 4, 304

BALLY TOTAL FITNESS

Chain of health clubs. Varying facilities may include fully equipped weight rooms, pools, and squash courts, aerobics classes and spa treatments. Call for locations.

☎ 800/846–0256

BURKE WILLIAMS DAY SPA & MASSAGE CENTER

Celebrity favorite for hedonistic beauty treatments from facials and pedicures to thermal seaweed wraps.

➕ Off map, west ✉ 1460 4th Street, Santa Monica ☎ 310/587–3366 🚌 4, 22

GOLD'S GYM

Home of the Gold's Gym world-wide body-building empire.

➕ Off map, west ✉ 360 Hampton Drive, Venice Beach ☎ 310/392–6004 🚌 33, SM1

GRIFFITH PARK GOLF

Two 18-hole and two 9-hole courses. Facilities include club rental, carts, proshop, dining, and night-lit driving range.

➕ Off map, northwest ✉ Griffith Park Drive, Griffith Park ☎ Information and reservations 213/485–5566 🚌 96

GRIFFITH PARK TENNIS

More than two dozen courts (available both day and night) at three locations. No reservations required for Griffith Park Drive courts.

➕ Off map, northwest ✉ Griffith Park Drive and Vermont Canyon, Griffith Park ☎ Information and reservations 323/485–5566 🚌 96

SANTA ANITA RACE TRACK

A lovely track in the lee of the San Gabriel Mountains. Thoroughbred horse-racing December to April, October, and November. Free viewing of morning workouts and weekend tram tours.

➕ Off map, northeast ✉ 285 W Huntington Drive, Arcadia ☎ 626/574–7223 🚌 79, 187, 188, 379

TENNIS PLACE

Midtown lighted tennis courts open late. Lessons available.

➕ M7 ✉ 420 S Grand Avenue ☎ 213/931–1715 🚌 DASH B

WORLD GYM

Another legendary workout facility (rivaling Gold's) for the Nautilus narcissists on Muscle Beach. Other locations in Pasadena and Burbank.

➕ Off map, west ✉ 812 Main Street, Venice Beach ☎ 310/399–9888 🚌 33, SM1

Jogging

LA's most attractive option is probably the 22-mile beach path running south from Santa Monica. Or try Exposition Park downtown; Griffith Park in the Hollywood Hills; and, just to the west, the great trail around quiet Lake Hollywood reached by car off Cahuenga Boulevard (via Dix Street).

Spectator sports

Catch the LA Dodgers (☎ 213/224–1400) at home at the Dodger Stadium, north of Downtown. The LA Lakers (☎ 310/419–3121) play the Forum, Inglewood; while the LA Clippers (☎ 213/748–8000) are at the Sports Arena in Exposition Park.

LUXURY HOTELS

Prices

The following price bands are given on a per night minimum, based (except for hostels) on two adults sharing a standard room:

Luxury hotels—over $150
Mid-range hotels—$60 to $150
Budget hotels—up to $60

(LA's 14 percent transient occupancy tax is added to the final bill).

Most hotels offer accommodations in several price ranges. If you are on a budget and the rate offered is at the top end of your limit, check to see if there is anything cheaper. Also note that many hotels negotiate on the price if they still have vacancies later in the day.

BEVERLY HILLS HOTEL
Legendary pink palace on 12 landscaped and palm-fringed acres.
Off map, west ✉ 9641 Sunset Boulevard, Beverly Hills ☎ 310/276–2251 or 800/283–8885 🍴 Two restaurants, coffee shop, poolside café ▣ 2

CHATEAU MARMONT
Castle-style 1927 favorite of Gable, Lombard, Harlow et al; John Belushi died here.
A2 ✉ 8221 Sunset Boulevard, Hollywood ☎ 323/656–1010, or 800/242–8328 🍴 Dining room with fine wine cellar ($$$) ▣ 2

HOTEL BEL-AIR
LA's finest tucked away in a wooded canyon.
Off map, northwest ✉ 701 Stone Canyon Road, Bel-Air ☎ 310/472–1211, or 800/648–4097 🍴 Fine restaurant ($$$)

HOTEL NIKKO AT BEVERLY HILLS
Sleek Japanese-inspired décor; 2-line speaker phones and large desks.
Off map, west ✉ 465 S La Cienega Boulevard, Beverly Hills ☎ 310/247–0400, or 800/645–5687 🍴 Excellent restaurant ($$$), Pangaea (▶ 63) ▣ 20, 21, 22

MONDRIAN
Ultrachic Ian Schrager/Philippe Starck co-production. Large rooms with scented candles, CDs, and city views.
Off map, west ✉ 8440 Sunset Boulevard ☎ 323/650–8999, or 800/525 8029 🍴 Restaurant ($$$), Sky Bar (▶ 81) ▣ 2, 3, 302

NEW OTANI
Luxury in little Tokyo. Rooms have Western beds or Japanese futons.
N7 ✉ 120 S Los Angeles Street ☎ 213/629–1200, or 800/421–8795 🍴 Three restaurants ($$–$$$), Thousand Cranes (▶ 65) ▣ DASH A

REGENT BEVERLY WILSHIRE
Sumptuous European-style grand hotel.
Off map, west ✉ 9500 Wilshire Boulevard, Beverly Hills ☎ 310/275–5200, or 800/427–4354 🍴 Excellent restaurant ($$$), The Dining Room (▶ 64) ▣ 20, 21, 22

RITZ-CARLTON HUNTINGTON
Beautifully restored 1907 hotel; luxurious facilities, stunning gardens.
Off map, northeast ✉ 1401 S Oak Knoll, Pasadena ☎ 626/568–3900, or 800/241–3333 🍴 Famous grill room ($$$)

SHERATON GRANDE
Fine Downtown hotel with oversize rooms, wall-to-wall windows and superb city views.
M7 ✉ 333 S Figueroa Street ☎ 213/617–1133, or 800/325–3535 🍴 Very good restaurant ($$$), and grill ($$) ▣ DASH A

SHUTTERS ON THE BEACH
Lovely rooms and suites in a New England-style edifice right on the beach.
Off map, west ✉ One Pico Boulevard, Santa Monica ☎ 310/458–0030, or 800/334–9000 🍴 Very good restaurant ($$$) ▣ 22, 33

MID-RANGE HOTELS

CARLYLE INN
Delightful boutique hotel with spa, fitness centre, free local shuttle, and complimentary breakfast buffet.

✚ Off map, west ☒ 1119 S Robertson Boulevard, West LA ☎ 310/275–4445, or 800/3–CARLYLE 🍴 Restaurant (SS) 🚪 220

CONESTOGA HOTEL
Old West-theme hotel; heated pool, game room, babysitting, free shuttle to nearby Disneyland.

✚ Off map, southeast ☒ 1240 S Walnut Street, Anaheim ☎ 714/535–0300, or 800/824–5459 🍴 Restaurants (S–SS) 🚪 460

CONTINENTAL PLAZA LAX
A comfortable airport bargain with pool and a more welcoming atmosphere than most.

✚ Off map, southeast ☒ 9750 Airport Boulevard, LAX ☎ 310/645–4600, or 800/529–4683 🍴 Restaurant (S)

FIGUEROA HOTEL— CONVENTION CENTER
Useful mid-range businessmen's hotel in central location.

✚ L8 ☒ 939 S Figueroa Street ☎ 213/627–8971, or 800/421–9092 🚪 DASH C, F

HOLIDAY INN HOLLYWOOD
Convenient for Hollywood Boulevard, clean and not too expensive. Pool and helpful staff.

✚ D1 ☒ 1755 N Highland Avenue, Hollywood ☎ 323/462–7181, or 800/368–9760 🍴 Restaurant (SS) 🚪 1, 217

HOLLYWOOD ROOSEVELT HOTEL
Refurbished Spanish Colonial-style Hollywood legend (► 53) with poolside cabana rooms.

✚ D1 ☒ 7000 Hollywood Boulevard, Hollywood ☎ 323/466–7000, or 800/950–7667 🍴 Good restaurant (SS–SSS) 🚪 1, 217

MALIBU COUNTRY INN
Romantic New England-style inn.

✚ Off map, west ☒ 6506 Westward Beach Road, Malibu ☎ 310/457–9622, or 800/386–6787 🍴 Breakfast included 🚪 434

PASADENA HOTEL
Turn-of-the-century b-and-b inn.

✚ Off map, northeast ☒ 76 N Fair Oaks Avenue, Pasadena ☎ 626/568–8172, or 800/653–8886 🚪 483, 485

UNIVERSAL CITY HILTON & TOWERS
Universal Studios packages, good family and business facilities. Pool. Kids under 18 stay free in parents room.

✚ Off map, northwest ☒ 555 Universal Terrace Parkway, Universal City ☎ 818/506–2500, or 800/HILTON 🍴 Restaurant (S–SSS) 🚪 420, 424, 425

ZANE GREY PUEBLO HOTEL
The Western writer's 1926 pueblo-style home on Catalina Island. Wonderful views; pool.

✚ Off map, southwest ☒ 199 Chimes Tower Road, Avalon ☎ 310/510–0966, or 800/3–PUEBLO 🍴 Breakfast included

Bed & Breakfast

Bed and breakfasts and private home stays are increasingly popular alternatives to hotels. Since 1978, Bed & Breakfast California (☎ 1-800/872–4500; fax 415/696–1699; e-mail info@bbintl.com) has offered a state-wide reservations service, and currently represents more than 300 historic homes, small inns, and private homes providing B&B accommodations in charming rooms or separate apartments.

BUDGET ACCOMMODATIONS

Location

This is a major consideration when choosing a hotel in a sprawling city like LA. Most hotels listed are on the main east–west transportation corridors between Downtown and the coast at Santa Monica. If your visit will last more than a few days, consider staying in a couple of different areas (Santa Monica and Hollywood, or Beverly Hills and Pasadena, for instance).

BANANA BUNGALOW HOLLYWOOD HOTEL/HOSTEL
Rooms and dorms; friendly, international atmosphere; free airport pick-up, beach and Disneyland shuttle, tour service, pool, movie theater, games room, laundry, kitchen, free parking.
➕ E1 ✉ 2775 W Cahuenga Boulevard, Hollywood
☎ 323/851–1129, or 800/4–HOSTEL 🍴 Restaurant (S) 🚌 420

BAYSIDE HOTEL
Great position across from the beach and one block from Main Street.
➕ Off map, west ✉ 2001 Ocean Avenue, Santa Monica
☎ 310/396–6000
🍴 Restaurants near by
🚌 4, 20, 22, 33, SM1, 7, 10

BEST WESTERN STOVALL'S INN
Large resort hotel close to Disneyland, mobbed with kids. Free shuttles to Disneyland and Anaheim, tour desk, children's menu, pool, Disney channel.
➕ Off map, southeast
✉ 1110 W Katella Avenue, Anaheim ☎ 714/778–1880, or 800/854–8175
🍴 Restaurants near by (S)
🚌 460

BEVONSHIRE LODGE MOTEL
Conveniently located between Farmers' Market and the Beverly Center. Pool; free parking; efficiencies available.
➕ Off map, west ✉ 7575 Beverly Boulevard, Midtown
☎ 323/936–6154
🍴 Restaurants near by 🚌 14

CITY CENTER MOTEL
Small and quiet hotel with pool, west of the I–110/ Harbor Freeway downtown.
➕ L7 ✉ 1135 West 7th Street
☎ 323/628–7141, or 800/816–6889 🚌 DASH E

DESERT INN & SUITES
Well-equipped rooms and good facilities close to Disneyland.
➕ Off map, southeast
✉ 1600 S Harbor Boulevard, Anaheim ☎ 714/772–5050, or 800/4333–5270
🍴 Restaurants near by (S), breakfast included 🚌 460

ECONOLODGE HOLLYWOOD
Handily positioned for Melrose Avenue and Hollywood sightseeing.
➕ E3 ✉ 777 N Vine Street, Hollywood ☎ 323/463–5671, or 800/446–3916
🍴 Breakfast included
🚌 10, 11

HOLLYWOOD YMCA
Dorms and excellent sports center off Hollywood Boulevard.
➕ D1 ✉ 1553 N Hudson Avenue, Hollywood
☎ 323/467–4161 🚌 1, 217

HOSTELLING INTERNATIONAL
Good-size hostel close to the Pier. Courtyard, laundry, library, tours, and activites. Some private rooms.
➕ Off map, west ✉ 1436 2nd Street, Santa Monica
☎ 310/393–9913 🚌 20, 22, 33, SM8

LOS ANGELES
travel facts

VIA RODEO
N. RODEO DR

ARRIVING & DEPARTING

Climate

- LA is mild and temperate and sunshine and fair weather is pretty much guaranteed from May to October. Humidity ranges from 65 to 77 percent. August and September can be unbearably hot and sticky and the smog is at its worst. The rainiest months are November to March.
- In summer, the heat is tempered by sea breezes. The beach can be fogbound until mid-morning—be patient and it burns off.
- In winter, 70°F days can be interspersed with 50°F nights; you may need a sweater or jacket after dark.
- For current conditions and forecasts, plus helpful travel tips, call the **Weather Channel Connection** from a touch-tone phone (95¢ per minute) ☎ 900/932–8437. LA Surf and Weather Report ☎ 310/578–0478

Arriving by air

- Los Angeles International Airport (LAX) lies 17 miles southwest of Downtown. It is the main arrival and departure point for both foreign and domestic flights. For information ☎ 310/646–5252
- To drive into the city centre from Airport Boulevard, take La Tiera Boulevard, then 1-405 through West Los Angeles.
- An alternative, possibly quicker, route is to take La Tiera Boulevard, then go north on La Cienaga Boulevard into West LA. La Cienaga intersects both Wilshire and Olympic boulevards, which run east through Downtown.

- Well-priced shuttle services to all areas of the city, such as SuperShuttle ☎ 800/554–3146 depart around the clock from the ground transportation island outside the lower level baggage claim area.
- The Metro Airport Service connects all eight terminals (Shuttle A), and the remote car parking lots (Shuttle B and Shuttle C). Shuttle C also serves the terminal for bus connections to the city.
- Cabs are readily available. Depending on traffic, the fare to Downtown or Hollywood is $30–$40.

Arriving by bus

- LA's main Greyhound/ Trailways terminal is Downtown ⊠ 1716 East 7th Street. There are also terminals in Anaheim, Hollywood, Pasadena, and Santa Monica.
- Information ☎ 213/629–8402 or 800/231–2222

Arriving by train

- Visitors and commuters enter the city through Union Station ⊠ 800 N Alameda Street, just north of Downtown, on the Metro Red Line and DASH shuttle bus routes.
- Information Amtrak ☎ 213/624– 0171 or US 800/872–7245.

ESSENTIAL FACTS

Money matters

- Nearly all banks have ATMs that accept cards linked to the Cirrus or Plus networks.
- For specific Cirrus locations in the United States and Canada, ☎ 800/424–7787. For Plus locations, ☎ 800/843–7587 and

enter the area code and first three digits of the number you are calling from (or of the calling area where you want an ATM).

- Credit cards, a secure alternative to cash, are widely accepted.
- An 8.25 percent sales tax is added to marked retail prices.
- Funds can be wired via **American Express MoneyGram** ☎ 800/926–9400 from the US and Canada for locations and information or **Western Union** ☎ 800/325–6000 for agent locations or to send using MasterCard or Visa ☎ 800/321–2923 in Canada

Etiquette

- LA dress is casual. Men are rarely expected to don a jacket or tie to dine in the smartest restaurant in town.
- Smoking is illegal in all public buildings, and is now banned in bars and restaurants as well. It is permitted in outdoor seating areas of restaurants, though do not expect your neighbors to be friendly about it. There are designated smoking rooms in many hotels.
- Tipping: 15–20 percent is expected by waiters; 15 percent for cab drivers; $1–$2 per bag for porters; and $1–$2 for valet parking.

Gay and lesbian resources

- LA is very gay-friendly. For general information and assistance, contact the Gay and Lesbian Community Servies Center ☒ 1625 N Schrader Boulevard, West Hollywood, CA 90028 ☎ 323/993–7400. See Magazines ➤ 92 for lesbian and gay publications.

Student travelers

- An International Student Identity Card (ISIC) brings reduced admission to many museums and attractions.
- Anyone under 21 is forbidden to buy alcohol and may not be allowed into some nightclubs.
- For written information about student services within the US, contact the Council on International Educational Exchange (CIEE) ☒ 205 East 42nd Street, New York, NY 10017 ☎ 212/822–2600 or 888/268–6245

Senior citizens

- Money-saving senior citizens discounts are available on a number of services as well as admission to attractions. Inquire ahead when booking hotels and car rentals. Take proof of age to ticket booths at theme parks, museums, and other visitor attractions to obtain discounted prices. Chain restaurants may also offer senior citizens discounts on certain menus, and early bird specials provide savings. For information about services and facilities for the elderly at Los Angeles International Airport (LAX), contact Travelers Aid ☎ 310/646–2270.

Time differences

- Los Angeles is on Pacific Standard Time (US West Coast), three hours behind Eastern Standard Time in New York, and two hours ahead of Hawaiian Standard Time.

Tourist information

- Los Angeles Convention & Visitors Bureau ☒ 633 West 5th Street, Suite 6000, Los Angeles, CA 80071 ☎ 213/624–7300. There are two Visitor Information Centers: Downtown Los Angeles ☒ 685 Figueroa Street (between Wilshire and 7th Street), Los Angeles, CA 90017 🕘 Mon–Fri 8–5, Sat

8:30–5; Hollywood ✉ The Janes House, 6541 Hollywood Boulevard, Hollywood, CA 90028 🕐 Mon–Sat 9–5; a multi-lingual events hotline ☎ 213/689–822 provides current information 24 hours a day.

- Long Beach Area Convention & Visitors Bureau ✉ One World Trade Center No. 300, Long Beach, CA 90831 ☎ 562/436–3645 or 800/452–7829 🕐 Mon–Fri 8:30–5

- Pasadena Convention & Visitors Bureau ✉ 171 S Los Robles Avenue, Pasadena, CA 91101 ☎ 626/795–9656 🕐 Mon–Fri 8–5, Sat 10–4

- Santa Monica Convention & Visitors Bureau ✉ 520 Broadway, Suite 250, Santa Monica, CA 90401–2428 ☎ 310/393–7593 🕐 Mon–Fri 9–5. Also Visitor Center ✉ 1400 Ocean Avenue ☎ 310/393–7593 🕐 daily 10–4

- Los Angeles Central Library ✉ 630 5th Street ☎ 213/228–7000 ➤ 56

PUBLIC TRANSPORTATION

- LA has a public transportation system operated by the Los Angeles County Metropolitan Transit Authority (MTA or Metro), though most Angelenos and visitors prefer the convenience and flexibility of a car, especially at night.

- Buses provide the most extensive coverage of the city. Limited subway (Metro Red Line) and light rail (Metro Blue Line) services are due to be expanded rapidly in the next few years. The Metro Green Line parallels I–105 from Norwalk west to El Segundo.

Buses

- The DASH Downtown shuttle bus service operates within the downtown Financial District, extending out to Exposition Park in the south, and north to Chinatown via Union Station and El Pueblo.

- The DASH operates every 5–15 minutes, Mon–Fri 6:30AM–6:30PM (some rates vary), for a flat fare of 25¢. Limited service on weekends. For more information ☎ 808–2273 (no area code required).

- The MTA bus services most useful to visitors are the main east–west routes from Downtown to Santa Monica, and north–south to the South Bay area.

- Buses operate daily 5AM–2AM, supposedly every 15 minutes, though services can be erratic. Outside these hours, reduced-service night buses ply major routes.

- The flat fare is $1.35 at the time of writing; transfers cost an additional 25¢. Have the correct change ready.

Metro rail services

- LA's proposed Metro system will revolutionize travel in the new millennium, but as yet its effects are minimal. Train services operate daily 5AM–11:20PM. To date the Metro Red Line subway extends from Union Station across Downtown and west on Wilshire Boulevard to Western Avenue. A link to Hollywood Boulevard/Vine Street is scheduled for late 1998.

- The Metro Blue Line between Downtown and Long Beach takes about 45 minutes, and services operate daily 5–10, with trains every 6–10 minutes in peak hours, every 15 minutes at other times.

Schedule and map information

- Schedules and maps area available from the MTA ✉ ARCO Plaza, 515 S Flower Street (Level C), Los Angeles ◉ Mon–Fri 7:30–3:30; ☎ 6249 Hollywood Boulevard, Hollywood ◉ Mon–Fri 10–6; ✉ Union Station ◉ Mon–Fri 6AM–6:30PM. Or ☎ 800–COMMUTE and the operator will tell you the best way to get from a to b ◉ Mon–Fri 6AM–8:30PM, Sat–Sun 8–6.

Taxis

- It is virtually impossible to hail a taxi on the street, except possibly Downtown.
- Hotels and transportation terminals are a good place to find a taxi, and restaurants will call one on request.
- Alternatively phone one of the following firms:
  Independent Cab Company ☎ 213/385–8294)
  LA Taxi ☎ 213/627–7000
  United Independent Taxis ☎ 213/653–5050

DRIVING

- The best way to get around LA is by car. Outside the main weekday rush hour periods (7AM–9AM, 3PM–7PM), the freeway network is generally a fast, efficient way of getting across town. The freeways at first seem like lethal five-lane racetracks, with overtaking on both sides and frequent lane-changing, but most visitors acclimatize quickly.

Car rental

- The main car rental companies have offices downtown as well as at LA International Airport.
- At the airport, they provide free shuttles to their parking lots from the ground transportation island outside the lower level baggage claim area.
  Alamo ☎ 800/327–9633
  Avis ☎ 800/331–1212
  Budget ☎ 800/227–7117
  Dollar ☎ 800/800–4000
  Hertz ☎ 800/654–3131
  Thrifty ☎ 800/645–1880

Freeway driving

- Always plan your journey in advance using a freeway map (basic versions are supplied by car rental companies). Note the exit, the direction of travel, and the number and name of the freeway; remember that the same highway may go by a different name in each direction.
- The *Thomas Guide*, a comprehensive street guide, is available at good bookstores.
- Details of freeway driving conditions are broadcast on radio stations KNX/1070–AM and KFWB/980–AM.
- The most frequently used freeway routes are:
  I-5 Golden State Freeway (north), Santa Ana Freeway (south)
  I-10 Santa Monica Freeway (west), San Bernardino Freeway (east)
  US-101 Hollywood Freeway (north/south)
  I-105 Century Freeway (west/east)
  I-110 Pasadena Freeway (north), Harbor Freeway (south)
  SR-134 Ventura Freeway (west/east)
  I-210 Foothill Freeway (west/east)
  I-405 San Diego Freeway (north/south)
  I-710 Long Beach Freeway

(north/south)
Another well-known route is the Pacific Coast Highway/US1 aka the PCH), which hugs the coast between San Diego on the south and San Francisco on the north via Santa Barbara.

Regulations and speed limits

- Seat belts are required; children under four must be secured in a car seat.
- It is legal to turn right on a red light, after making a full stop, unless other wise posted.
- Pedestrians have right of way at crosswalks. Californians take this rule of the road very seriously—far more seriously than elsewhere in the US. Be sure to look for pedestrians before turning right on red.
- At four-way crossings without traffic lights, in law, cars cross in order of arrival at the intersection; if two cars arrive simultaneously the car to the right has priority. In reality, it is he who dares that wins.
- Freeway car pool lanes can be used by any car carrying the requisite number of passengers (generally two or three), indicated by signs posted at the freeway entrance.
- Unless otherwise posted, the speed limit is 55 or 65mph on urban freeways; 35mph on major thoroughfares; 25mph on residential and other streets.

MEDIA & COMMUNICATIONS

Telephones

- Local calls cost 20¢.
- LA has a number of local telephone codes. Some calls within the LA area require more than a 20¢ deposit. Dial the number and a recorded operator message gives the minimum deposit.
- The area code for Downtown Los Angeles is 213; other useful area codes include 323 (the area immediately surrounding Downtown and Hollywood); 310 (Beverly Hills, Westside, Santa Monica); 562 (Long Beach, and other South Bay areas); 626 (Pasadena); 818 (San Fernando Valley).
- Calls from hotel rooms are far more expensive than those from public phones.

Post offices

- Post offices are generally open Mon–Fri 8:30 or 9AM to 6PM, Sat until 1 or 2PM.

Newspapers

- LA's only major English-language daily newspaper is the *Los Angeles Times* (local and international news).

Magazines

- The free *LA Weekly* has an excellent listings section with a guide to clubs, music venues, and arts events.
- There are numerous free magazines and other gay-orientated publications, such as *Frontiers* and *Edge*, which provide listings, local events, and entertainment updates.

Radio and television

- LA's airwaves hum with everything from jazz to "shock jocks" to Spanish language and religious programs. KROQ-FM 106.7 one of the best rock stations in the US; also KSCA-FM 101.9. There are golden oldies on KACE-FM 103.9;

classical on KCSN-FM 88.5; and jazz programs on KLON-FM 88.1 and KCRW-FM 89.9.

- In addition to national network channels, many hotels have cable TV, pay-per-view movies and the Welcome Channel, a visitor information broadcasting service.

EMERGENCIES

Sensible precautions

- Few visitors ever see LA's high-crime areas, the South-Central district and East LA.
- Venice Beach is unpleasant after dark, infested with drunks and drug peddlars.
- Anybody, particularly lone travelers and women, should be careful and avoid unlit and unpeopled areas after dark.
- Always plan your trip in advance, and consult your car rental agency or hotel staff, or call your destination to make sure of the exit you want.
- To foil pickpockets, do not carry easily snatched bags and cameras, especially in busy areas.
- Carry only as much cash as you require.
- Don't leave anything of value in cars, even when it is concealed.
- Most hotels provide a safe where you can leave valuables. Use it.
- Report lost or stolen items to the nearest police precinct (see Lost Property) if you plan to make a claim.

Lost property

- LA International Airport: contact your own airline and ask for its lost-and-found

department.
- Airport police ☎ 310/417–0440
- MTA (Metrobuses and Metrolink) for lost property ☎ 213/937–8920
- Otherwise call the relevant police precinct; addresses and phone numbers are listed in the phone book.

Medical treatment

- Many hotels can arrange for referrals to a local doctor or dentist. Or look under "Physicians and Surgeons" or "Dentists" in the *Yellow Pages*.
- Most city hospitals accept emergency cases. Those with well-equipped 24-hour emergency rooms include: Cedar-Sinai Medical Center ✉ 8700 Beverly Boulevard, West Hollywood ☎ 310/855–5000 and Good Samaritan Hospital ✉ 1225 Wilshire Boulevard, Los Angeles ☎ 323/977–2121

Medicines

- Pharmacies are plentiful; look in the *Yellow Pages*.

Emergency telephone numbers

- Fire, police or ambulance ☎ 911 (no money required)

Consulates

- Australia ✉ Century Plaza Towers, 19th Floor ☎ 310/229–4800
- Denmark ✉ 10877 Wilshire Boulevard ☎ 310/443–2090
- Germany ✉ 6222 Wilshire Boulevard ☎ 213/930–2703
- Netherlands ✉ 11766 Wilshire Boulevard ☎ 310/268–1598
- New Zealand ✉ 12400 Wilshire Boulevard ☎ 310/207–1605
- Sweden ✉ 10880 Wilshire Boulevard ☎ 310/441–3763
- UK ✉ 11766 Wilshire Boulevard ☎ 310/477–3322

INDEX

Citypack
Los Angeles

Copyright	© 1997, 1999 by The Automobile Association
Maps copyright	© 1997, 1999 by The Automobile Association
Fold-out map:	© RV Reise- und Verkehrsverlag Munich · Stuttgart
	© Cartography: GeoData

Published in the United States by Fodor's Travel Publications, Inc.
Published in the United Kingdom by AA Publishing

Fodor's is a registered trademark of Fodor's Travel Publications, Inc.

ISBN 0–679–00249–9
Revised Second Edition

FODOR'S CITYPACK LOS ANGELES

AUTHOR *Emma Stanford*
CARTOGRAPHY *The Automobile Association*
          RV Reise- und Verkehrsverlag
COVER DESIGN *Fabrizio La Rocca, Allison Saltzman*
ORIGINAL COPY EDITOR *Moira Johnston*
REVISION VERIFIER *Emma Stanford*
INDEXER *Marie Lorimer*
SECOND EDITION UPDATED BY *OutHouse Publishing Services*

Acknowledgments
The Automobile Association wishes to thank the following photographers for their assistance in the preparation of this book: The Armand Hammer Foundation 26a; Gene Autry Western Heritage Museum 33b; Rob Holmes 55b; The Hulton Getty Picture Collection Ltd 12; The Huntington Library 46; J. Paul Getty Museum 25a, 25b; Los Angeles County Museum of Art 28; Photos courtesy of Los Angeles Convention & Visitors Bureau/ C 1995 5b, 6, 7, 13a, 30b; Museum of Neon Art 51(Lili Lakich); Norton Simon Art Foundation 45b; Petersen Automotive Museum 29a, 29b; Pictures Colour Library 24a, 37b; Rancho Los Alamitos 43; © 1996 The Walt Disney Company 48. The remaining pictures are held in the Association's own library (AA Photo Library) and were taken by Phil Wood with the exception of pages 19, 36, 49b, 60 which were taken by Rob Holmes.

Color separation by Daylight Colour Art Pte Ltd, Singapore
Manufactured by Dai Nippon Printing Co. (Hong Kong) Ltd
10 9 8 7 6 5 4 3 2 1

Titles in the Citypack series
- Amsterdam • Atlanta • Beijing • Berlin • Boston • Chicago • Dublin •
- Florence • Hong Kong • London • Los Angeles • Miami • Montréal •
- New York • Paris • Prague • Rome • San Francisco • Seattle • Shanghai •
- Sydney • Tokyo • Toronto • Venice • Washington DC •